A Story About Pizza

By
Erica D'Arcangelo

Copyright © 2024
All Rights Reserved

978-1-917327-00-8 (Hardcover)

Dedication

I dedicate this book to my father. When you spoke, I listened.

Foreword

Fleeing from a life of poverty, exploitation, and violence, over 4 million Italian men, women, and children immigrated to the United States from Italy. The largest time span was between the years of 1880 and 1924.

There were 2 million Italian immigrants in the 10 years between 1900 and 1910 alone.

After a hard-earned trip across the Atlantic Ocean, many washed up along the shores and subways of the East River in New York by way of Ellis Island.

Some were diseased. Others starved and famished. But, most of them were looking for a new life. This dramatic surge of immigration, accurately called "The Great Arrival," was just the beginning.

The long trip to *La America* was hard-won. Faced with multitudes of challenges this group of artisans, farmers, and laborers fought for jobs necessary to take care of their families.

Today Italian-Americans make up the fifth largest ancestral group in the United States. Italian culture has molded America with our obsession with art, fashion, and food. But most of all, Italian culture has given new meaning to family, tradition, and loyalty.

I should know. I grew up in an Italian family. My grandparents were from the town of Lanciano, in the Region of Abruzzo, Italy, born in the Italian Province of Chieti bordering the Adriatic Sea. My father is 100% Italian.

But this isn't a story about me, immigration, or Italy. This is a story about my grandfather, a man named Pietro Americo, and his love of family and pizza.

Note: This is an adaptation based on a true story.

Table of Contents

Dedication ii

Foreword iii

Chapter 1 The Long Journey 1

Chapter 1 Recipe Focaccia Bread 9

Chapter 2 Welcome to New York 11

Chapter 2 Recipe Pizzelle Cookies 19

Chapter 3 Home Away from Home 20

Chapter 3 Recipe Homemade Pasta 31

Chapter 4 Windber 32

Chapter 4 Recipe San Marzano Tomato Sauce 36

Chapter 5 The Mines 37

Chapter 5 Recipe Italian "Miner's" Hoagie 45

Chapter 6 Days and Years 46

Chapter 6 Recipe Steak & Pea Stew 53

Chapter 7 The Family Home 55

Chapter 7 Recipe Wedding Cookies 60

Chapter 8 Justino D'Arcangelo 62

Chapter 8 Recipe Italian Braciole Sauce Recipe ... 65

Chapter 9 The Berwind-White Coal Company 67

Chapter 9 Recipe Meatballs 70

Chapter 10 D'Arc's Market 71

Chapter 10 Recipe Pizza Frittas 78

Chapter 11 D'Arc's Pizza 80

Chapter 11 Recipe Anna's Polenta 90

Chapter 12 The Shop + The Pizza Oven..........................91
Chapter 12 Recipe Ravioli's..95
Chapter 13 Family..97
Chapter 13 Recipe Pete's Sausage and Peppers 104
Chapter 14 A Windber Tradition 105
Chapter 14 Recipe Emery's Pasta Fagioli 110
Chapter 15 The Big Move...112
Chapter 15 Recipe Homemade Bread............................119
Chapter 16 A Part of Life...120
About the Author 122

A STORY ABOUT PIZZA

Chapter 1
The Long Journey

As the church bells rang to announce that it was noon Pietro looked up. Suitcase in hand, and rushing through the streets of Lanciano, Abruzzo he saw all of the familiar sights and sounds of home.

The cobblestone road. The smell of bread, cheeses, meats, and seafood from the local shops.

Bikes traveling up and down the streets carrying familiar faces. Intoxicating smells of food from local shoppers, wrapped and stored in bike baskets as they pedaled past him.

Stray cats sitting outside the market waiting for a drop of fish or a spilled drink, or even some soggy bread laid out by the shop owners at the end of the day.

Usually Pietro would stop for a few minutes to take it all in. He would grab a piece of day-old focaccia from the local bakery, tearing off a small piece for his favorite tabby cat, feeding him and getting a friendly pat on the head in return. He would watch the old couples as they argued in Italian about what shop to go to next. Best of all he would close his eyes as he smelled all of the food, dreaming of his next meal, or better yet, a slice of authentic homemade pizza.

But not today.

Today Pietro was in a hurry. There was only time for one stop: his favorite local bakery for that one slice of pizza.

"Andiamo," yelled his father. "Hurry, hurry, let's go!" While his mother gently pushed him and his three brothers down the cobblestone road. "Andiamo ragazzi," she said as she gently guided them down the street.

Usually Pietro made the journey there on his bike from the farm where he lived with his family. He ordered his slice and sat outside on the stoop enjoying every bite and then feeding one of the stray cats the last of his crust.

Pietro had just turned ten years old. He stood tall for his size, slender, with sandy brown hair and light blue eyes. His skin tone was lighter than most of his Italian family members, as his features mirrored those of his father.

Pietro's face also had quite a few freckles which became more prominent the longer he was in the sun.

On this busy morning the pizzeria was packed. Pietro, his father, mother, and brothers Domenick, John, and Alfred hustled in. "La tua pizza migliore la prendiamo noi," said Pietro's father. "We'll take your best pizza."

After what seemed like an eternity, with a growing hollow in his stomach, Pietro and his family got their pizza. The owner, Luigi, also gave his father a bag of focaccia.

"Addio amico mio. Viaggia in sicurezza ("Goodbye my friend. Travel safely)," he said as the family of six hustled out the door and back out into the busy street.

As they made their way into the crowd, Pietro's mother handed each boy a slice of pizza. "Fa caldo stai attento," she said. "It's hot, be careful." But Pietro never worried when it came to eating hot pizza, or any pizza for that matter.

From the smell of the pizza to the first bite Pietro's mouth watered.

A STORY ABOUT PIZZA

Traditional Margherita pizza was his favorite with fresh San Marzano tomatoes and fresh grated mozzarella. And, what pizza could be complete without a little bit of Parmigiana. Pietro could eat pizza every single day, for every meal. He thought about how pizza was made, picturing the ingredients, and how his pizza was cooked at the pizzeria. Crust turning a golden brown, cheese bubbling, and that crispy sound of the pizza being cut right in front of his eyes.

Within a few seconds, his slice was gone. Pietro could have eaten more pizza but he knew he needed to move faster. He walked quickly down the street with his suitcase in his hand still daydreaming about the fresh slice he had just devoured.

Before he knew it, Pietro and his family were boarding a boat. "Do you have everything?" Pietro's father asked his mother in Italian. With a quick, careful glance around she replied, "Si."

Pietro's stomach, although not completely satisfied, was full enough from his last slice of pie. He decided to take a nap. He would have the focaccia later.

Pietro was eager to start his new life and for his mother and father to finally be able to settle down. He yearned for a home, and a permanent place to call his own. He dreamed of the day where he could wake up in his own house with his family and not have to watch his parents fight about not having enough work, money, or food. A safe place where he could find refuge.

A safe place where he could find refuge. As much as he loved Italy, he knew that if he and his family stayed there they would face a more difficult life than if they left.

The stress was weighing on his mother and, most of all, his father who had grown more and more angry and resentful as the days and weeks passed before they left.

The sun was shining brightly when Pietro closed his eyes but as he dreamt, it grew dark. His dream was vivid. He was walking through the field in Lanciano. There was tall grass everywhere and it felt like the closer to his home he walked, the further from home he got.

As Pietro slowly opened his eyes from his slumber, he felt hot. The boat was rocking from side to side and the cabin was full. Families huddled together, babies crying.

Everything felt damp. His stomach growled. How long had he been asleep? It was also dark other than the small lanterns being held up around the cabin.

He glanced around and saw his parents, both fast asleep. He gazed at their faces. His father, Justino, was a tall, skinny, bald man with a shadow on his face. The hair he had left on his head was light brown with spots of gray, and freckles covered his arms and lightly sprinkled his face.

Pietro's father looked tired. From the first moment Pietro could remember, Justino was always working manual jobs that involved intense physical labor. He would return home, exhausted and sometimes hurt. Soft spoken and reserved, he would eat his dinner and go to sleep, preparing himself for the next day, the next job. However, Justino also had a short temper and often took his frustrations out on his wife, Anna. Particularly after he drank.

Pietro's mother was a petite Italian woman with dark hair and eyes.

A STORY ABOUT PIZZA

She often wore her hair clipped up with a scarf wrapped around it. She always wore a dress with long stockings underneath and a shawl as she was frequently cold. Anna was a devout Catholic and a member of the local church. She attended mass whenever she could and prayed for the family, particularly Justino.

With the boat far out in the sea, Pietro's brothers were huddled together dreaming. Domineck was stout and a bit gruff in his looks. He was quiet but kind, and caring. Physically, Domenick was the largest of the four boys. Though he was quiet, he liked to argue more than anyone else in the family. Domenick was not one to back down from any conflict or fight which often left Pietro to bail him out, even though he was smaller and not as strong as his older brother.

Alfred looked more Irish than Italian to Pietro. He had red hair and freckles, and was the baby of the family. He looked most like his mother of the four sons. Alfred was incredibly loyal to his family and to his brother Pietro. He was also sarcastic and was the one in the family that kept all the boys laughing. Even Justino, who Pietro had never seen laugh, would crack a smile if the mood allowed him to.

John looked a lot like Pietro and Justino with well-defined Italian features but he alone of all the boys had his mother's eyes and hair color. Domenick and Pietro were the oldest. John and Alfred were younger, and the older boys often grew tired of their bickering. Of all four sons, Pietro was also the quietest and most reserved.

Out of the corner of his eye, Pietro saw the bag of focaccia near his mother's hand and moved his hand slightly out to grab a piece. He put his hand in the bag and pulled out a nice square of focaccia. The first bite was salty but perfect. He tasted the fresh olive oil. Pietro wondered if he would ever eat focaccia like that again in America.

After he enjoyed his midnight snack Pietro went back to sleep. He awoke the next morning to the hustle and bustle of the travelers. Many conversations in Italian, the smell of coffee and salt water. The cabin was very dark at night, but if the weather allowed the doors were open in the morning and the first of the morning light poured in with the smell of the salt water in the air. Although it was not heated, the amount of people in the cabin and closed doors caused the area to be stuffy all night, but at least slightly warm so the travelers didn't freeze.

"Buogiorno," said Anna to the four boys and Justino. All four boys nodded. Justino was silent and clearly unhappy with the trip thus far. He ignored Anna and looked ahead.

One of the mothers of the other families had a bag of Italian cookies which she shared with Pietro and his brothers. After the boys finished eating, Pietro became curious. He was a few feet from his brothers, who were standing alone, unsure of where to go.

"Andiamo" said Pietro. "Let's go." It was time to explore the boat and he figured he might as well take them both along. "Domenick, do you want to go?" asked Pietro. Domenick nodded his head *no* as he picked up an old, dirty booklet that he saw nearby and started looking at it.

Pietro and his brothers went up the stairs and opened a heavy door. The light was so bright they all squinted and covered their eyes. After the initial shock of the light hit them they continued up to the main deck. Water surrounded them. The boat was smaller than they had hoped. But the sea was never-ending. The boys walked up and down the main deck, breathed in the fresh salt water air, and hoped at some point soon they would be able to see land.

Little did they know they were only one day into a very long journey. The first day went by fast and all three boys were tired from exploring. They fell fast asleep early in the evening.

As the cabin got lighter, Pietro opened his eyes again. But this time it was much later in the journey.

How many days had he been here? It seems like at least 100. The cabin appeared to be fuller than before.

The same babies were crying. Or were they different ones? Pietro didn't know or care at this point. He was hungry. He thought about his last piece of focaccia. Would he ever eat again?

"I'm hungry," whispered Pietro to his mother Anna. "I know, my love," said Anna. "Have patience. We will be there soon enough."

Pietro was trying but was getting impatient with his brothers' bickering and fighting. Pietro was quiet, and normally didn't complain. Neither did Domenick. But the two younger boys were weighing on everyone's patience.

"Shut up, John," said Alfred. "No, you shut up," said John, shoving him. Justino briefly got up and grabbed both boys and shoved them to the ground. He turned around to Anna and grabbed her by the arm.

"If you don't keep these boys in line, I will," he said. Anna grimaced in pain and shrunk back not saying a word. Both boys sat still glaring at one another but not making any moves toward each other.

Pietro walked away from his family in the cabin and went up the stairs again. Maybe some fresh air would do him some good. The boat was rocking more than usual the last few hours and he felt somewhat queasy.

As Pietro made his way up the stairs he noticed the door was locked. Why couldn't he go upstairs? He peered out the small window and saw that the main deck was soaked. He could barely see two feet in front of him. It seemed as if the boat had hit some rough water.

Pietro sulked back into the cabin where he waited for three more days. His mother had rationed their food and they were coming down to the last of it. A family of six, even eating just one meal per day, hardly had enough.

He glanced around the cabin at the back wall. That's where the sick were quarantined. Pietro was happy he at least wasn't stuck with the sick travelers who were without their families. But he was young. Nevertheless, he and his family were tired and ready for the trip to end. The food would be running out soon.

The dream of a new life never left Pietro. All he could do on this long trip to America was think about what things would be like for him and his family. He hoped that it would be similar to Italy, at least the food part, but mainly that his father would be afforded more opportunities and his family could finally feel settled and at peace. They had struggled for long enough.

Little did Pietro know, this struggle was only the beginning. But often, when young people don't see outside of their dreams. Maybe that was a good thing for Pietro.

A STORY ABOUT PIZZA

Chapter 1 Recipe
Focaccia Bread

Ingredients

For the Dough

2 cups of organic unbleached bread flour

1 pack fast rise yeast

1 teaspoon of salt

1 cup warm water

To Garnish

1 teaspoon of salt

1 teaspoon of pepper

½ cup olive oil

½ cup parmesan cheese

Toppings of your choice could include tomatoes, fresh garlic, rosemary, or whatever you want to add to it.

Our traditional recipe is plain focaccia with salt, pepper, and a little parmesan.

Directions:

Add the flour to a large bowl or mixer. Hollow out the middle and pour in the pack of fast-rising yeast. Turn on the mixer and start to add in the hot water until the dough starts to mix. You may not need it all but may need more. The dough should be sticky, but not watery. Mix it for a few minutes until it's slightly sticky but not liquidy. If your dough is too wet add in more flour. If it's too dry, add in more water.

Stop mixing and cover. Let it raise for at least 1 hour.

Now it's time to roll the dough. Add flour to your counter or rolling space. Grease a pan with olive oil and roll your dough to a consistency of around ½ inch or so. Add it to the pan. Cover and let rise for another 20-30 minutes.

Use your fingers to poke holes in the dough and add your olive oil to the top. Sprinkle with salt, pepper, and parmesan cheese. Bake for 8-12 minutes in the oven set at 425 degrees Fahrenheit.

# Chapter 2
Welcome to New York

Pietro woke up very slowly that morning. The weeks of traveling had worn on him. He wasn't sure how long he'd been there but it was about three days since he'd eaten anything. His clothes were dirty, and he was uncomfortable. Even though he wanted to, Pietro didn't complain.

His mother always could see when he was unhappy, and assured him it would be okay. He glanced over to see her looking at him with an encouraging smile. Just that alone comforted Pietro.

"Are you thirsty, my loves?" Anna asked the four boys. All of them nodded yes. Anna took out some water she'd been saving and told them to pass it around. Each boy from oldest to youngest took a gulp. This made Pietro's stomach growl even more but, at this point, he didn't even care.

When his eyes scanned the room, he also noticed something else. The dark basin of the boat where he and the other families lived was lighter. All the doors were open. He smelled the air and it smelled different than before.

There was also something else. The boat wasn't rocking. It was barely moving at all. Pietro jumped up and grabbed his small bag of items. His family was stirring and he started to nudge them all awake telling them to look at the light.

Pietro then saw families walking up the steps. He wanted to run. He couldn't wait to race to the top, but he didn't want to get lost. So he patiently stayed with his family as they grabbed their belongings. As they walked up the steps onto the main deck of the boat, Pietro felt wonder and excitement about what he would see.

Much to his surprise and delight, as he walked to the deck of the boat, he saw the harbor. It was filled with boats.

As he looked on he saw huge buildings and people everywhere. "Americo," he said. "We're here."

"We're here, we're here," yelled Alfred and John. Domenick looked around carefully but didn't say a word.

"New York," said Anna as she gazed in awe. Justino was quiet.

Pietro and his family stepped off the boat onto land. Now they had to wait in line. Paperwork and health checks were done. It seemed to take hours.

Even though his stomach was growling, Pietro didn't care. There was just so much to see. So much to take in.

Pietro gazed in awe at the giant buildings, the automobiles, and the crowded streets. It was his first time in a city, and he immediately fell in love with the sights, the smells, and the people.

After the medical checks his family were finally free. They met up with Justino's brother Angelo and headed off to stay at Angelo's house.

"Hello, brother," Angelo said to Justino. "Ciao, fratello," said Justino as he shook his brother's hand.

"Hello boys!" bellowed Angelo. "My boys are in America. All of my boys," as he hugged his four nephews, all of whom tried to get away unsuccessfully.

A STORY ABOUT PIZZA

Angelo was a short, dark-haired man with brown eyes. He wobbled a bit when he walked as he was a bit overweight. Although his hair was thinning he was still quite young. Angelo had a very big personality in comparison to his brother Justino who was much more quiet. When he spoke he nearly yelled and flailed his arms all over the place.

Growing up, Justino had always been more serious. He grew concerned about the present challenges in his life and was seemingly consumed with the hardships he faced in his life. Angelo, on the other hand, didn't seem too bothered and was almost jolly about his future. Though it was not easy for either brother, Angelo kept things into perspective that he could always change the things he was not happy about.

"Lighten up, brother," said Angelo as he slapped Justino in the back. "You're in America now. Time to lighten up".

Pietro and his brothers found their "Zio" [Uncle] Angelo humorous. They often chuckled when they saw Angelo talking to their very reserved father, Justino, who seemed to be uncomfortable with Angelo's over-the-top hand gestures and boisterous voice and tone.

Before heading to Angelo's home, the family made one stop at the local Italian pizzeria. They ordered a pie and Pietro noticed it was a bit larger and thinner than his traditional Italian pizza.

"This is the best pizza in New York," said Zio Angelo. "A real New York slice." Pietro nodded his head but he didn't care. He loved pizza.

Besides, he and his family hadn't eaten in days.

When the pizza came out the family stood around a small round table and each person took a slice. Pietro bit into his slice, not even bothering to worry about burning his mouth. The pizza was more delicious than it was hot. It had a perfectly browned crust, bubbling cheese, and red sauce. Pietro ate the entire slice within seconds.

He and his family walked to Zio Angelo's house where his wife Maria had beds laid out on the floor and couches made up for the entire family. As soon as Pietro walked into the door he smelled anise. His Aunt Maria had made a traditional Italian cookie called a pizzelle.

"Oh my boys!" she yelled as she cried tears of joy. "I'm so happy you're finally here."

Maria was a tall, slender woman with a beehive hairdo and black-rimmed glasses. She often wore house dresses and slippers and smelled like anise and vanilla.

Maria was very affectionate and smothered Pietro and his brothers with hugs and kisses as soon as they walked in the door. As they scrambled to get away they wiped their faces. Maria embraced Anna and Justino.

"Welcome, welcome," she said. "It took you long enough to get here. Now, let's eat."

As he walked out of the kitchen, Pietro grabbed a cookie while his mother ran a bath for him and his brothers.

Maria had set up the bathroom for the family where they had a white claw-foot tub. She described in great detail to the entire family how she had boiled water and spent the afternoon filling the tub as she waited for them to arrive..

A STORY ABOUT PIZZA

Anna would bathe first so she could help Maria in the kitchen. Then Justino and the boys. The water was black after the family bathed but they were able to change into some clean clothes. While Pietro and his brothers got ready, Anna helped Maria set the table for dinner then proceeded to the laundry tub to wash the family's clothing.

Anna collected the dirty laundry so she could wash all the clothes together. Justino, still quiet from the trip, had seemingly been happier since he arrived to Angelo's and Maria's home and was now having drinks with his brother.

While everyone enjoyed themselves Anna worked. She was a good wife and always made sure the boys and Justino were well fed, even with the little food the family had, and that they had clean clothing. She cleaned the house, cared for the family, and never complained. Anna dreamed of a better life like the rest of the family. She was quiet like Pietro except for when she sang softly in Italian as she did her daily chores.

Even though it was just a few short hours since he had last eaten, Pietro was hungry again. Thankfully his Aunt Maria was a gifted Italian cook. She had homemade tomato sauce on the stove and had made spaghetti for the family along with her famous bread.

That along with a few cheeses and some lettuce with olive oil and vinegar made for one of the best meals Pietro had. He also managed to get a few more pizzelles after cleaning his plate.

Over the next few hours the family ate, talked and laughed. Justino and Anna spoke of their long journey to the United States and their hopes for a better life.

Angelo talked about how he had set up his and Maria's life in New York while he worked as a shoe smith. The two had not had any children yet but were planning on it now that they were settled in America and planned to stay in New York.

The family also spoke about Italy, their parents, and what had happened in the old country. While Italy was one of the most beautiful places in the world the country had fallen into rural poverty and crime.

"I never planned to stay in the United States but at that time, there was more opportunity for me here and it was safer for my family," said Angelo.

"You have to go where there's work," replied Justino. "You have to go even though you don't want to."

The entire family agreed that they wished they could have stayed in their country; in their homes. Now both families had embarked on new lives where they needed to find suitable work, and make enough money to support themselves. They both planned to send money back to Italy for relatives that were still there.

Like many Italian immigrants, both families feared for the health and safety of their loved ones in Italy, but they had to migrate.

Angelo loved the city of New York, the people, and the other Italian immigrants. While they were not wealthy, they saved enough to give Justino enough money to travel six hours southwest by train to the next state. Many Italian immigrants from Lanciano, Abruzzo had gone there for work and it was the place that Justino wanted to take his family to start a new life.

A STORY ABOUT PIZZA

Pietro and his brothers wanted to stay in New York but Justino was the head of the family, and the boys listened to him. While he was a loving father, none of the boys nor Anna dared to cross him. Justino, while quiet and reserved, could turn angry and violent if challenged. Especially when he was drinking.

Justino lacked patience and, if pushed, became abusive to Anna and the boys. He was the hardest on Domenick and Pietro because they were the oldest.

That night, with his entire family sharing a small room Pietro slept well for the first time in a long time. He would be able to stay with his Zio for three more days before he had to go on another journey to a place where he hoped he could call home.

Over the next few days Pietro and his family finally got the well-deserved rest they needed. And of course, Pietro was able to eat pizza. He explored the city of New York with his family, quietly taking it all in.

Before he knew it, it was time for Pietro, his three brothers, and his mother and father to make yet another journey to what he hoped would be his permanent home. Thankfully, this journey would only take hours this time, not weeks.

Justino had accepted a job as a laborer at the Berwind-White Coal Company just outside Pittsburgh in the state of Pennsylvania. Pietro and his brothers would attend school. Anna would be a homemaker taking care of Justino and the four boys.

After the three days in New York had passed Pietro was up before it was light outside. He put together his belongings and headed out the door with his family. His Uncle Angelo walked them to the train station in New York.

A few families piled in together just about to take off on yet another long trip. Justino and Angelo embraced and Angelo wished the family luck.

"Thank you, my brother," said Justino to Angelo.

"Of course," replied Angelo. "Family is blood."

The two brothers embraced again quickly. They would see each other again. Pietro hoped it would be soon.

Pietro's brothers Alfred and John were both crying. But Pietro and Domenick didn't cry. Pietro was always hopeful that his final destination would be a place he could call home. Domenick didn't show emotion easily.

Much bigger than the other three boys, Domenick was nearly as tall as Justino, and stout. He was quiet but didn't fear his father as much as the other boys. Domenick was also likely to be more argumentative than the other three.

As Pietro climbed the tall steps into the train car he took one last look around New York. He sat down quietly and rested his eyes. There was not much else to do on his next journey but to sleep and to dream. And dream of his new life, he would. His dreams would also be filled with pizza; as they always were.

Chapter 2 Recipe
Pizzelle Cookies

Ingredients

4 cups of flour

1 cup of oil

1 ¼ cup of sugar

6 eggs

4 teaspoons baking powder

For the Flavor

2 teaspoons of vanilla, anise, or maple extract

Directions:

Add eggs, sugar, and oil and beat for several minutes on low. In a separate bowl mix flour and baking powder. Pour the liquid batter into the flour mixture. Beat until you get a texture that is a thick semi-liquid paste (about 2-3 minutes). Spoon batter onto a hot and oiled pizzelle iron.

Chapter 3
Home Away from Home

As the train stopped, a door opened and a fresh breeze blew through the car. The air smelled fresh and clean. Pietro took a deep breath. It was the end of summer but it felt a little bit chilly outside.

"Are you cold?" asked Anna. Pietro and Domenick shook their heads no, but Alfred and John grabbed a blanket from Anna's hands.

They briefly fought over it until Justino glared at them and they stopped.

Pietro wiped the fog from the window and peered out.

He saw lush woods, green trees and a dirt road. He also saw a lot of train tracks and coal carts filled to the brim. It was early in the morning. Dew lay on the grass and there was some fog. It wasn't time to get out yet but he was in a line and up ahead, families were stepping off the train.

About an hour later Pietro and his family had inched up to the front of the line and it was time to step off the platform. Justino helped Anna down while Pietro and his brothers jumped from the last step. All three landed on their feet on the dirt road.

Other families formed in a group and a transportation truck from Berwind-White pulled up and the families piled in the back. After about a thirty-minute drive the D'Arcangelo family arrived in Windber, Pennsylvania.

A STORY ABOUT PIZZA

The family grabbed their suitcases and continued walking. Standing about 100 feet down the road, was a man with a dark hat and coat on. He stared at all four of the boys with a glare before looking at Justino and Anna. Pietro didn't like the feeling he got from this man so he stepped behind his father and pulled his younger brothers in to stand closer to him.

Domenick didn't seem to notice him or care much.

"Justino?" said the man.

"Si," said Justino. "It's nice to meet you."

The man shook Justino's hand and handed him some papers and keys. He pointed to a house about fifty yards away. Justino thanked him and the family made their way in that direction.

"I am Lorenzo and I'm the Manager of Berwind-White Coal Company. I'll be your supervisor," the man said.

Lorenzo had immigrated from Italy two years earlier.

The family continued to walk down the dirt road toward the house. There were five small houses that all looked the same.

Each one had two floors with two windows on the second floor and a small porch in the front with a door.

The houses looked dirty and stained from the coal mines but Anna could take care of that.

Justino looked at the paper that said 111. Pietro matched the number to the number on the house. This was his house. He wanted to run to the door but he let his father lead the way. Pietro knew not to run ahead of Justino, especially into a house where he had never been.

As they made their way up the stairs, Pietro noticed some broken wooden boards on the porch. Justino used the key he had gotten from Lorenzo and the door creaked open slowly. Inside the house was cold, dark, and dirty but to Pietro it looked like home. He knew his mother would have it clean in just a matter of time.

Downstairs there were two small rooms: a kitchen and a living area. Up the steps were two more rooms. One room was a bedroom for Pietro and his brothers; the other for Justino and Anna.

Anna had already started to take note of all the things she would need to do to the house. Justino had one thing on his mind: starting his job with Berwind-White Coal Company the next day.

"Boys, help your mother clean up your rooms," said Justino. "I don't need help," said Anna. "Boys, just bring down any dirty laundry from upstairs so I can get a wash bucket started."

Alfred and John raced up the steps pulling each other down while Pietro and Domenick got dirty laundry from their suitcases and put it downstairs for Anna.

Justino lit a fire in the old coal stove in the kitchen used to both cook and heat the home.

Within minutes the home started to warm up.

While Justino spent the rest of the day looking at his work papers, Anna got to work. She found water and filled a bucket in the backyard. Thankfully there was a little soap. Anna washed a few of the blankets that were in the house and hung them on a line in the backyard so they could dry.

A STORY ABOUT PIZZA

After Anna finished with this she swept and scrubbed the floors and windows. Pietro and his brothers tried to stay out of the way but helped when their mother asked.

All four boys were careful not to set Justino off or upset their mother.

Justino left the house early in the afternoon to have a meeting at Berwind-White Coal Company. He came back a few hours later, just before dark, with some vegetables he had been gifted from one of the neighbor's gardens.

As Justino walked into the house he was staggering and slurring the few words coming out of his mouth. He reeked of booze.

"Here," he said. "From the neighbor and I had to drag them the whole way back here for you."

Anna very quietly used the gas stove and cooked the vegetables along with some pasta that had been sent by their Aunt Maria.

Justino had also been given some local bread that he aggressively broke into pieces which he threw toward each family member.

The entire family ate in silence, terrified not to set Justino off since he had been drinking.

Anna had picked the dry, clean blankets off the clothes line earlier and told the boys to make the beds.

By dark, the house was clean. The beds were made. All of the family was fed and everyone was tired. Pietro was happy to be spending his first night in the home, as were his brothers.

While upstairs the boys heard their father yelling in the kitchen at their mother.

"You shut up and do what I say," said Justino. "You're no good, no good for nothing. It took you all day to clean this house and this meal was terrible."

The boys heard a thud and a scream as Anna was pushed across the room.

After that the house was silent.

Later, with a rag wrapped around her arm and her eyes swollen from tears,

Anna came in to tuck the boys in and tell them a very quick story about her adventures in Italian when she was a girl in Italy.

This story made all of the boys interested in exploring their woods, the entire area around their house, and the mines, and seeing what was in store for them.

As Anna spoke her voice cracked a bit. Pietro and Domenick glanced at each other and then down. The younger boys didn't seem to notice much of anything at all.

Domenick, Alfred, and John were already asleep before Anna left. Pietro was still awake. His mother asked him if he liked the house and Pietro said, "Yes."

"Are you ok?" asked Pietro as he looked at his mother's arm with concern.

"I'm fine, my love," she said, holding back tears. "You go to sleep now and tomorrow is another day."

She quickly kissed him goodnight and went off to bed.

A STORY ABOUT PIZZA

Pietro couldn't fall asleep at first. His mind was going at a million miles per hour thinking about his mother, the future, and what his life could be in this small coal mining town.

He couldn't wait to explore the new place and see what it had to offer. He also hoped that his mother would be safe here and that in some way, his father would find some kind of happiness.

Pietro wondered if the new town was anything like his home in Italy.

He hoped that he could find pizza that tasted even remotely like the pizza he had at the forno near his home. Or even that pizzeria near his Zio's house in New York.

Before he knew it, Pietro had fallen into a deep sleep. He dreamt of Italy. Riding his bike through the streets, stopping to pet the stray cats and feeding them the crust from his pizza. His dream started to change into him walking on a street in Italy to sudden darkness and then walking down the dirt road in America. He could see New York from afar and, as he continued walking toward the buildings and the city they got further and further away.

As the light hit his face, he felt a cool breeze and woke up. How was it already morning? His mother was in his room and had opened the windows. Pietro smelled toast. Probably from some of the leftover bread from the night before. He also smelled eggs.

"Boys, it's time to get up," said Anna. "You're going to school."

Pietro was surprised. "School, already?" he said.

"Yes, now get up and get ready," she said.

She had laid out all three boys' clean outfits for them.

Domenick, Alfred, and John rumbled around and rolled out of bed. They got dressed and headed to the bathroom pushing each other gently out of the way.

Pietro then got up and got himself dressed. His brothers had finished in the bathroom and Pietro got ready and went downstairs. All four of the boys had their egg and toast.

Justino had found out the day before that the school was only about 200 feet up the road. Anna walked there with the four boys. After a conversation in Italian with the teacher all three boys went in and sat down. The teacher spoke Italian but many of the books were in English so Pietro and his brothers would need to learn English.

The school was a small yellow brick building with two brown metal doors at the front. Small windows lined the outside walls of the classroom where, when the children gazed out, they could see rows of trees. Across the street were some local shops that were just being built.

Alfred and John, who were younger than Pietro, didn't seem to mind the school, or the fact that they had to learn English. Pietro was worried he would never be able to learn but knew that he would need to try if he was going to survive in his new home. Domenick had the same fear but would never let anyone know it.

The school day went by fairly quickly. Most of the boys' classes were in Italian and they had started to learn a little bit of English even on the first day.

When the final bell rang the teacher told the boys she would see them tomorrow. Pietro grabbed a book and his

A STORY ABOUT PIZZA

brothers and started walking home. When he got there he saw that Anna had cleaned up the house even more and unpacked all the suitcases from the trip.

In just two days their house was already starting to look like a home.

"Okay boys, how was your first day?" asked Anna.

John and Alfred spoke at length about their teacher and books and what they had learned. Domenick and Pietro said 'bene' in unison and went upstairs. Domenick was older than the other three boys and knew it would be a matter of time until he went to work in the mines. Pietro wanted to be alone and reflect on the day and his new home.

Despite the older boys wanting to be alone, they didn't have a lot of time to themselves that day after school; or any day for that matter. Each of them had a chore to attend to when they got home from school.

Pietro had to sweep the fireplace hearth and cut some firewood. The weather, even though it was late summer, was starting to get chilly, especially when the sun went down.

Alfred and John were in charge of setting the dinner table which they bickered about the entire time, pushing each other and arguing without concern as their father was still at work.

Eventually the boys settled down and finished their chores. The fireplace was swept. The table was set. Anna had managed to get a few groceries from the local Eureka Company Store, which she called the market, and was cooking a small dinner for the family.

Tonight it was more pasta that they had from Aunt Maria, vegetables, and beans that Anna made into a tomato-based soup called pasta fagioli.

Anna and the boys waited for Justino to get home. When he walked in he looked tired and was covered in black coal soot. He went to wash up and sat down at the table with his family.

Alfred and John started to bicker and Justino became agitated rather quickly.

"Stop it," said Pietro. "Knock it off now."

Just as the words came out of his mouth Justino stood up and hit Pietro in the face.

"All three of you knock it off," he screamed.

The two boys cowered in fear as Pietro ducked, covering his head while completely silent.

Pietro wished he was as shocked and scared as his brothers but this had happened before. He knew to remain silent so as to not further agitate his father. Anna looked upset. She remained quiet. Justino sat back down and finished his dinner. He got up abruptly and went upstairs and went to bed.

The boys slowly sat back down at the table and finished their dinners. Even though the pasta fagioli had gotten cold, it was still good.

After they and Anna finished eating, Anna washed and put away the dinner and dishes without saying a word. Pietro inspected his wound. His face was red, but not bruised. He washed up and went to his room.

"Pietro," called Anna gently.

A STORY ABOUT PIZZA

As he came down the steps, his mother handed him the same cold rag she had used on her arm the previous night.

"Hold this on your face until the stinging stops," she said. She then gave him a gentle kiss on his forehead. "Now go upstairs."

She was holding her rosary in her right hand, pProbably to pray for Justino after what happened.

Alfred and John were looking at a book they got from school and quickly fell asleep. Pietro opened his book and started reading. He stopped for a minute to think about what had happened at dinner. Pietro wondered why his father attacked him the way that he did.

He wished that he would stop and vowed to never do that to anyone. While Pietro loved his father, he never knew where he stood with him. Pietro was careful to not upset him or react when Justino got upset with him or Anna.

But, inside, Pietro was frustrated and angry. Why did his father have to do this? What could he do to stop it?

Pietro couldn't wait to get older and bigger so he could fight back. He wanted to protect himself and his mother.

He wanted to tell Justino he was a coward to pick on his wife and children who loved him. Most of all he wanted to talk to his mother and tell her it would be ok. But for now, all he could do was wait, hope, and pray for more time before it happened again.

Pietro also felt somewhat resentful of his brothers. Why did he always have to protect them? Why didn't they understand that they couldn't fight in front of his father?

He wondered why Domenick never stuck up for him, his mother, or his brothers. He was nearly the same size as Justino.

Pietro would talk to them later. It was late. Frustrated, Pietro finally fell asleep.

Chapter 3 Recipe
Homemade Pasta

Ingredients

3 eggs

3 cups of flour

A pinch of salt (1 teaspoon)

A pinch of olive oil (1 teaspoon)

Directions:

On a clean counter, table or in a large bowl dump in the flower. Hollow out the middle and add the eggs there. Drop in the salt and olive oil. Hand mix until you have a dough-like consistency. If your pasta is too dry add an additional egg or 1 more teaspoon of olive oil. If it's too wet, add in additional flour.

Make a ball with the dough and wrap it on plastic (or put in a container with a lid). Let it rest in the fridge for at least 30 minutes.

Add flour to a clean surface and get the dough out. Roll it thin on the surface. Cut by hand based on how thin you want your noodles. Drop into a well-salted pot of boiling water and boil for 3-4 minutes until al dente. Serve with your favorite homemade sauce.

Chapter 4
Windber

When Pietro opened his eyes it was still dark outside. He heard his mother walking around the house and his father rustling awake. What day was it? Pietro didn't think it was a school day but wasn't sure since everyone was up so early.

He heard his mother's footsteps coming to his and his brothers' room.

"Get up and get dressed," she said.

Pietro and his brothers slowly got out of bed and ready. When they walked downstairs, both parents were standing by the door ready to go. Anna told the boys to put their shoes on.

The air was chilly as the family walked out to a wagon filled with other families from the mines. Where were they all going?

Pietro reluctantly got in. He was cold. As the sun came up Pietro saw that the leaves on the trees were starting to turn colors. It was fall.

The carriage took the families to the train station. After purchasing some tickets they boarded a train.

"Where are we going?" Pietro asked.

"The market," she replied.

Pietro fell asleep and woke up just as the train was stopping. He and his family had traveled about two hours on the Pennsylvania Railroad to the city of Pittsburgh.

A STORY ABOUT PIZZA

When Pietro stepped off the train he took a deep breath. He smelled the city. Better yet, he smelled food and pizza.

The family walked away from the station to a row of streets filled with vendors. Anything Pietro could ever want was there as he gazed in awe at the fresh bread, cheeses, meats, and fish vendors around him speaking Italian. For a brief moment, Pietro found himself back in Italy.

His brothers were not as excited about walking around the market as Pietro was. They pouted as they marched behind Pietro, Anna, and Justino with their heads down lightly pushing each other. Both were careful to hide from Justino because of what had happened the night before.

Pietro's stomach growled after the family got some cheeses, bread, and meat. Then they stopped for lunch at a pizza vendor who told the family he had been up since 3:00 a.m. cooking fresh pizza and focaccia bread.

The family enjoyed a slice of pizza, and Anna purchased some focaccia to have the following week. The pizza was as good as Pietro remembered it from the last time he had it. It was warm with a thin crispy crust, just enough cheese, and tomato sauce.

The family had very little money but they had saved just enough for one slice each plus the focaccia bread to take home. After they picked up some flour they headed back to the train station and sat on a bench.

Anna gave each of the boys one small piece of focaccia bread to hold them over. It was warm and perfectly salted. Pietro wondered if the baker was from the same town as him, in Italy.

Families rushed to the station and headed to the train as it was about to depart. Everyone in the cabins seemed happy with the market and the trip.

About an hour into the train ride Pietro gazed out the window at the mountains and leaves. It certainly was beautiful, but it wasn't Italy. Still, he felt at home there.

Maybe this was where he was meant to be.

As all the families left the train and got into the truck to go home, Pietro wished that every single day could be like the day he just had. Although he didn't mind school, he loved the sights and sounds of the city. He loved the food. Most of all he loved that his family could spend a day together without his father being angry. Where he could get away and experience life, just like he had been taught to do in Italy by his grandfather.

Pietro dreamed that night of the market. He was back on the train looking out the window. He was walking around the crowded streets and taking in all the smells of the local vendors' food.

When he woke up he smelled his mother's homemade tomato sauce. Tomatoes were in season and plentiful during these months and Anna was wasting no time picking, cooking, and canning them for the upcoming winter. The family would attend Catholic mass that morning and then have Sunday dinner.

Pietro and his brothers put on their best pants, suspenders, and shirts and headed to church. As he stood next to his mother Pietro made sure that his brothers were paying attention during mass and not fighting with each other. During the sermon he saw Alfred pinch John out of the side of his eye and looked at

A STORY ABOUT PIZZA

them both with a stern glare. Both boys stopped and looked forward, paying attention to the rest of the mass.

After church the family walked home together quietly. When they entered their home it smelled amazing. Anna had been cooking tomato sauce since early that morning and had made homemade spaghetti. The D'Arcangelo's sat down to Sunday dinner and they had the spaghetti with some more of the bread from the market the day before.

Everyone seemed happy, forgiving, and content including Justino who kissed Anna on the cheek kindly and thanked her for the delicious meal.

Chapter 4 Recipe
San Marzano Tomato Sauce

Ingredients

1-2 pans of San Marzano tomatoes (about 50)

4-5 cloves of fresh garlic

2 teaspoons of salt

1 teaspoon of pepper

Fresh basil and oregano (about ¼ cup each chopped)

2 tablespoons of olive oil

Directions:

On a lightly oiled pan add clean tomatoes. Drizzle with olive oil, salt and pepper. Roast tomatoes at 400 degrees for 40 minutes.

Take the tomatoes out of the oven and let them cool. Peel the skin off the tomatoes. Crush the tomatoes by hand or by using a food processor or blender.

Add 1 teaspoon of olive oil and fresh garlic to a large pot and summer. Add in the crushed tomatoes and a little salt and pepper. Bring to a boil then put on low and let simmer. Add in the fresh basil and oregano.

Serve with your favorite pasta. The D'Arcangelo recommendation is plain spaghetti with Parmesan Reggiano and hot pepper seeds sprinkled on top.

Chapter 5
The Mines

During their first years in America, Pietro and his family developed a routine in their new home. Justino went to work in the Berwind-White coal mines every day with Domenick. Pietro, Alfred, and John went off to school. Anna took care of the house, the meals, and the family. She attended Catholic mass every Wednesday night and Sunday morning and was often found praying with her rosary in hand.

They weathered the seasons which came and went from the beautiful fall leaves to the freezing cold winter. Then spring came as everything thawed and grew again, leaves appearing green on trees and flowers blooming.

Before they knew it, it was summer again.

The winter months were tough on everyone but mainly Justino. He had to weather the storm while working in the mines daily and dealing with the elements along with the safety issues of working in the coal mines. The boys and Anna were careful not to disturb him when he came home. Justino came home black from the mines. Anna boiled water and had a bath waiting for him. Anna also cleaned the soot from his clothes and shoes and kept the house clean from it.

After what seemed like a never-ending winter, spring came again and Pietro and his brothers could not have been happier. They played outside after school. The sun went down a bit later and came up earlier. Everyone, even Justino, seemed to be in better spirits.

Summer would be coming again soon. This was the D'Arcangelo family's favorite season. The days were longer with the warm sun shining in through the trees and every night there was a cool breeze where they could hear the leaves rustling in the wind.

After dinner the miners and their families would sit out on their porches.

Sometimes Justino would take his boys for a walk around to other miners' homes to chat and enjoy the weather. Domenick and Pietro would always walk with their father while Alfred and John would run ahead and play.

Pietro wondered if he would ever have a summer in America like his summers in Italy. The never-ending days where he walked around town, fed the cats, and visited the markets. Sampling the local foods (mainly the pizza). How he had enjoyed chatting with the store owners and their families and waving at shoppers on bikes weaving in and out of foot traffic on the stone and brick roads!

During the day Pietro still dreamed about this from his school desk as he looked out the window. He looked forward to warm weather and longer days.

Before he knew it, school was out and the sun was shining. Pietro enjoyed a few days playing in the woods with his brothers and picking berries so that Anna could make a pie. He and his brothers would return home muddy and cut from blackberry bushes, with their mouths and fingers stained from picking and their bellies full from eating more berries than they could count.

Domenick started working in the mines with Justino just after school got out. He returned home daily with his father

A STORY ABOUT PIZZA

tired and quiet, having dinner and retreating to bed somewhat resentful that he couldn't enjoy his summer.

Just as Pietro was settling into his summer routine things took an unexpected turn.

As Pietro came into the house one night ready for dinner both of his parents were sitting at the kitchen table.

"Pietro," said Justino. "Vieni qui. Come here."

Pietro slowly and cautiously walked into the kitchen and sat down with his mother, father, and brother Domenick. Anna looked upset.

"You are going to work in the mines with your brother," said Justino. "The mines need more workers and its time to earn your keep. You start tomorrow."

Pietro answered, "Si padre," as he felt a burning anger and disappointment. Domenick nodded his head and walked away quietly as if it didn't bother him at all. It was as if he knew or was expecting it all along.

Pietro didn't want to work in the mine. Not now. Not ever. He didn't want to be like his father. Unhappy every day, arriving home exhausted, and never having the energy to spend time with anyone or just be happy.

"Why didn't you tell me?" said Pietro to Domenick. "At least let me know what I'm walking into."

"We both have to go there," said Domenick. "You think I like it any more than you do? Just don't make a big deal about it. You're not a kid anymore."

As strong as Pietro's desire was to not work in the mines, his desire to please his parents was stronger. He was not going to let them see his disappointment. Pietro was getting older and would be paid a stipend for working. If nothing else he wanted to contribute to his family and help take care of them.

As much as he hated it, Domenick was right. Pietro understood he wasn't a kid anymore. He stopped grumbling to himself and got his clothes ready for work the next day.

The next morning Pietro got up early with Justino and Domenick, and they went off to work in the mines. Anna sent them all with lunches and kissed Pietro before he walked out the door holding back tears. She did not want her eldest sons to work in the mines either. But Pietro knew what he had to do. There was no way around it.

When he arrived at the mines Pietro was told that his job would be to clean off slate from the coal before it was shipped. He was working with twenty other boys right around his age. Some he knew from school. The team of boys were called "breaker boys." When he arrived at the place they were stationed many of the boys waved.

Pietro was well-liked. Even though he was quiet, he made it a point to know everyone's name and a little bit about them so he could chat with them.

The first day of work was long. There was very little time for breaks. Pietro ate his lunch quickly. His hands were black and fingers sore by the end of the day. He came home. bathed. and went straight to bed exhausted. At least he had some friends to talk with while he worked all day.

The next morning Pietro got up again with Justino, and Domenick to go to work. As he sat up from his bed he looked over at Alfred and John. He was jealous of them both as they were peacefully sleeping after a day of playing in the sun.

A STORY ABOUT PIZZA

As Pietro walked out the door, Anna gave both her sons hugs.

"I'm proud of you both," she whispered.

Tears welled up in Pietro's eyes, but he was not about to feel sorry for himself.

"Thank you, mama," he said.

This was a part of growing up. Besides, a little hard work never hurts anyone.

During the day Pietro was quiet. He did his job and listened to the other boys talk and joke, chatting with them from time to time. Even though Pietro didn't want to work in the mines he never complained.

However, if Pietro ever had to describe the mines he would say they were a "black hell." The conditions in the mines were unsafe. They were dark and dirty with tunnels and long drops. Men got hurt often from falls, explosions, and miner's lung where the dust from the mines would get into their lungs causing them to hack and cough.

Justino had had the coal miner's cough for some time now, and this greatly worried Anna and the boys.

Pietro worked above ground for now with the rest of the crew, although some were called to dig up coal from narrow tunnels that the grown men could not fit into.

While working in the mines, Pietro spent a lot of his time observing Justino. His father was a foreman in the mines with Lorenzo. Before this time, Pietro had always been fearful of his father's temper, the way he would treat his mother and brothers if they spoke at the wrong time or said the wrong thing.

However, after Pietro saw his father next to Lorenzo he realized that Justino's behavior was mild in comparison.

Lorenzo walked around the mines as the lead foreman. Everyone there was afraid of him. He threatened the miners and especially the young boys, instilling fear while constantly berating and abusing the other workers.

The breaker boys were particularly afraid of him. When he wasn't around some of the boys would tell a story about how Lorenzo threw a boy down a mine shaft.

Pietro didn't know if it was true or not. He did know that he wanted to stay as far away from Lorenzo as possible, and wanted the same for his father.

Something else happened to Pietro while working in the mines. For the first time in his life, Pietro had compassion for his father instead of hate. In the years leading up to this, he had considered his father to be somewhat of a monster. But now he was starting to understand why Justino behaved the way he did.

After the first few weeks of working in the mines, Pietro had adjusted. He had accepted the conditions of the mines. He had learned how to stay clear of Lorenzo.

Pietro had even made friends with the other breaker boys. For the first time in his life he had also bonded with Justino and Domenick, with the three of them even chatting in Italian during dinner about the other workers and miners' politics.

Pietro noticed a shift with his father where he also switched from disciplining him and Domenick to correcting

A STORY ABOUT PIZZA

his younger brothers which both slightly pleased and somewhat worried Pietro at the same time.

Pietro loved and protected both Alfred and John fiercely. He was also somewhat jealous of their carefree youth.

Their obliviousness when it came to noticing how hard Justino, Domenick, and now Pietro worked and how tired they were at the end of every day. The way that they bickered and fought got under Pietro's skin.

Domenick was a closed book. Much like Justino, Pietro could never quite read him. He spent a lot of his time off work drinking at the local Abruzzi Club with some of the older breaker boys.

Even on Sunday after mass Domenick would start pouring himself Coffee Royale's around noon. After he had a few drinks in him, he often got into fights with the other miners. Justino would always show up to bail him out.

And even though Justino would never admit it, Pietro could see that his father was proud of him and Domenick, despite the problems Domenick got himself into.

His mother, never being able to hide anything easily, went from sadness and despair every morning when they went off to work, to pride. Pietro never complained.

He understood that no matter what happened in his life he was responsible for where he was at and changing it.

In the short time he was in the mines, Pietro knew he would not work there for the rest of his life. For now, his small weekly stipend would go to his family. Later he would save.

Before he knew it, summer ended. Pietro knew that he was not going back to school before his father told him.

"You'll both be working in the mines this fall," said Justino to Pietro and Domenick.

Both boys nodded silently, briefly glancing at one another for a reaction that never came.

A STORY ABOUT PIZZA

Chapter 5 Recipe
Italian "Miner's" Hoagie

Ingredients

2 slices of homemade Italian bread or roll

4 slices of hard salami

2 slices of ham or Prosciutto

2 slices Capicola

1 piece of Mozzarella cheese

¼ cup shredded iceberg lettuce

2 slices of fresh tomato

Drizzle of oil and vinegar

Sprinkle of salt and pepper

Directions:

Add the meat to the bread or roll. Then add the cheese. Once that's done, add the lettuce and two tomatoes. Sprinkle it with salt and pepper.

Sprinkle the lettuce with a drizzle of olive oil and vinegar.

Wrap sandwich and store in a cool dry place.

Chapter 6
Days and Years

The first step to any unwanted situation is acceptance of what it is. Pietro didn't want to work in the mines. But he knew that was what he needed to do now to help his family.

As he grew older, the days and years of mining work didn't tire him. It made him stronger. The quiet thought sharpened him mentally. The physical labor changed him and made him more confident. He appreciated the friendships with the other miners. The structure and the schedule helped him mature.

While he didn't want to work in the mines for the rest of his life, he knew he had to make the best of the situation while he figured out how he was going to build a life outside of this.

For Justino, this was it. He would work in the mines for the rest of his life. Pietro wanted more.

After spending many months as a breaker boy, Pietro asked to do other jobs in the mine which he accepted.

Domenick had also moved up the ladder. He silently worked and came home never complaining.

Pietro's next job would be hauling coal where he had to navigate both the danger of the mines underground and the elements outside.

As time went on the conditions inside the mines became more deplorable.

The winters were freezing cold. Going underground in the mines was a death trap. The imminent dangers of getting caught in an explosion or trapped underground lurked

A STORY ABOUT PIZZA

everywhere. Pietro had to wear a handkerchief around his face to avoid coal lung, caused by breathing in the fumes.

While breathing underground was a challenge, working outside in the winters was likely worse. Pietro would arrive home with his hands frozen and blistered, filthy and exhausted. Even the blood from his hands froze during the day.

Justino was similarly drained from working in the mines and from the consent stress of Lorenzo and the deterioration of his lungs from the fumes.

Justino, Domenick, and Pietro arrived home each day black from coal. They quietly washed up, ate dinner, and went to bed.

The men worked in the mines six days per week.

Between them, they made very little money; weekly stipends for Domenick and Pietro and a meager foreman salary for Justino.

As bad as the conditions were, the abuse was worse. Justino would get into physical altercations from time to time with workers. Pietro feared retaliation and kept his head down and mouth shut.

Domenick didn't seem to notice or care. He seemed to fight for his own personal sport, especially after he had a few drinks. Sometimes Pietro would wonder what was going through his mind but realized the drinking and fighting might have been how Domenick dealt with things.

Lorenzo was the most feared and abusive foreman in the mines. His imagined threats were worse than any real danger he thought he was in. Anyone who crossed him was dealt with in the most violent manner possible.

For years, Pietro stayed clear of him. But, as careful as he was, Pietro could not avoid the wrath of Lorenzo.

As he was bringing a cart of coal up through the tunnel, the wheel broke. Coal spilled everywhere. Pietro desperately tried to pick it all up before anyone saw what happened. It was too late.

Lorenzo, observing this, marched over to him screaming, "You think you can do whatever you want here because your father is a foreman."

Pietro replied, "No, sir. The wheel broke. I apologize and will clean it up." At this point, he could feel the fear rising up from his stomach as his hands started to shake. He stopped for a moment and told himself to just clean up the mess and look at the ground.

"I'm sick of you thinking you own this place," said Lorenzo.

Pietro was bent down picking up the coal as quickly as he could. Before he knew it Lorenzo had picked him up and threw him against the wall of the mine. He punched Pietro in the left eye, and threw him on the ground.

As soon as Pietro hit the hard coal-lain floor Lorenzo kicked him three more times before walking away in a huff. Pietro covered up and didn't move at first.

He lay on the ground still in shock about what had occurred. His head was throbbing and when he lifted his hand to touch it, it was wet with blood. After a few minutes Pietro sat up. Other miners had gathered around him to help him. Domenick handed him a handkerchief to wipe his head.

A STORY ABOUT PIZZA

"You good?" asked Domenick. "Here, wipe your head. Get up. You're fine. Brush it off."

Pietro took a few deep breaths and stood up, feeling dizzy. After a few minutes, he was still dizzy, and the other miners helped him pick up the coal. He loaded it back into the cart and took it up to the top.

When Justino saw him, Pietro could see the initial shock and concern on his face that he quickly hid. In the mines, Justino could not go to Pietro and console him.

All three men finished their day and walked home in silence. Pietro's head was stained with blood. His face was bruised.

When his mother saw him coming up the driveway there was no way to hide the shock and horror on her face.

She ran to Pietro, crying.

"My son, what happened?" she asked. No one answered her.

"What happened to him?" she asked.

"Nothing, he had an accident," said Justino. "He'll be fine."

"He's fine," said Domenick.

Anna ran back into the house and got him a wet rag. SheAnna wiped his face and cleaned up the blood. She then told Pietro to go and wash up before dinner.

As the family sat down, no one said a word. They ate the stew Ana had made in silence. After dinner, Pietro went straight to bed, but he couldn't sleep. He heard his mother and father arguing in Italian.

"I'm taking the boys to New York for a few days," said Anna.

"You are not going anywhere," said Justino. "This happens. He's fine."

"He's not fine," said Anna. "Did you see his face?"

"Enough, Anna," said Justino. "Stai zitto or you will be next." Justino slammed his hand down on the table and kicked a chair. He raised his hand, but did not hit Anna. He turned around and stormed out of the room. Pietro could hear his mother weeping quietly, so as not to disturb his angry father.

The next morning Justino, Domenick, and Pietro got up and went to work in silence. They never spoke about what occurred in the mines between Pietro and Lorenzo.

Over the next few months Domenick decided to buy a small house. He moved out of the family home, but was still working in the mines full time.

Every Sunday Domenick would join the family for dinner after Sunday mass. As usual the D'Arcangelo men were quiet as they enjoyed their food after church while Anna chatted with them.

After a few minutes of silence, Domenick spoke as he sipped his Coffee Royale.

"I'm joining the service," he said.

"What?" said Anna. "When are you leaving?"

A STORY ABOUT PIZZA

"Tonight," said Domenick. Anna looked shocked as she made eye contact with Justino quickly and then looked down. Her eyes welled up with tears as she continued to clean up quietly.

Anna didn't want any of her boys to be far away from her, although she wasn't sure if the service would be any better for her son than the mines. She was somewhat relieved for Domenick to be out of the mines once and for all.

"Have you told the mines?" asked Justino.

"Yes," said Domenick. "I have to get there right away to enlist. I'll be back after basic training. Can you keep an eye on my house?"

"Si," said Justino. "Si."

Domenick hugged his mother and shook his father's hand. Then he left. As he walked out the door he nodded at Pietro and his other brothers.

Domenick hated working in the mines a much as Pietro did. He just never told anyone.

The next few weeks, conditions got worse in the mines.

More and more miners had accidents and abuse incidents than ever before. Justino and Pietro both heard rumblings from the other miners. The situation was growing more and more serious by the day and the miners had enough.

Over the next few months Pietro, Justino, and the other Italian, Polish, Slovakian, and Hungarian immigrant miners would strike as they sought to become members of The United Mine Workers of America.

Up until that point miners from mines 36, 37, 40, and 42 had been completely separated. Because they spoke different languages the mine companies felt they could better control the workers and prevent them from unionizing, and continue to pay them low wages.

As this union formed, the miners finally earned well-deserved rights.

Lorenzo was removed from his position at the mine and both Pietro and Justino were able to earn a fair wage for the first time.

Over the years, immigrants, who were recruited into the mines with promises of a better life, were faced with abuse, unfair wages, and unacceptable conditions. This all ended after the strike and formation of the union to protect miners' rights.

It could not have come at a better time.

After this period of enslavement, Pietro had renewed hope. Hope for better conditions. Hope for better wages. And, hope that no matter what he went through he could never give up on his dreams.

A STORY ABOUT PIZZA

Chapter 6 Recipe
Steak & Pea Stew

Ingredients

1 lb of steak (cut into small pieces) or beef stew cubes

1 yellow onion

1-2 cloves of garlic

1 bag of peas (or 4 cups)

8-10 potatoes (peeled cut)

1 can of tomato paste

1 16 oz can of tomato sauce

2 cups beef broth or water

1 tablespoon salt

1 tablespoon pepper

1 tablespoon of olive oil

Directions:

In a large pan, brown steak with olive oil, garlic, and diced onion until meat is slightly brown. Add in 1 can of tomato paste and saute with steak, onion, and garlic. Then add in the tomato sauce and stir. You can add water or broth to the mixture by using it to clean out the sauce and paste cans.

Drop in the raw, cut potatoes, salt, and pepper, and stir. Cover and bring to a boil then leave on low to medium heat until the potatoes are soft. Add in the peas (a bag of frozen peas usually works best). Put the stove on low and cover for at least an hour.

Serve stew with homemade bread.

Chapter 7
The Family Home

As Pietro opened his eyes, he couldn't help but to feel grateful. He still worked in the mines but he finally was able to earn some money which he stashed away hidden under his mattress.

Both Alfred and John were happy. His mother seemed pleased and proud. Domenick had written the family a very brief letter saying he was doing well in the service, but not much else.

Even Justino was in good spirits having been promoted and running the mines. After a long life of struggling, Justino, for the first time, felt more at ease. Growing older, Justino struggled with health issues, having been diagnosed with black lung because of his many years in the mine.

However, he stayed working there as he was finally earning money in the mines after years of enslavement.

His family was happy for the first time in years. Alfred and John were able to stay in school and finish their basic education.

As a boy turns into a man he creates his life with his own family. One Friday night out in Windber with his fellow miners, Pietro met a girl named Nicolette. Her family had immigrated from a small village in Italy called Cheiti in the Abruzzo region.

Nicolette was 5'4" with black curled hair and glasses. She came from a big family with one sister and two brothers. Nicolette was a talented cook with a sharp tongue. Her sarcastic wit, sense of humor, and loyalty to her family were the qualities Pietro loved most about her.

Nicolette spent most of her time outside of school helping in the kitchen and learning to cook. And what an amazing, gifted cook she was.

With better conditions on the horizon, Pietro started to dream about the next steps in his life: marriage, children, and how he was going to stop working in the mines.

But before he could do that Pietro had an important project to do with his father. Justino had taken his earnings from working in the mines, and bought a piece of land. Pietro, Alfred, and John were helping Justino build a family home.

The next weeks and months of Pietro's life would be full of more hard work. Not just his work in the mines but building a house by hand with his father and brothers.

After the land was prepared and measured, Pietro worked on the foundation with Justino. Once that was completed, Justino wanted the house to be built using stone. The boys would wheel the wheelbarrow up to the woods to the stone crusher, chisel the stones, bring them down, and cut them to put on the house.

"There aren't enough stones," said Justino. "Go get more now."

"Dad, there are enough," said Pietro.

"Don't make me tell you again," Justino yelled back.

"Let's go," said Pietro to John and Alfred. Both boys followed as they grumbled to each other resentfully.

A STORY ABOUT PIZZA

This lasted for months. Hands bloodied and back aching, Pietro never complained. Since he was the eldest son now at home, Justino was incredibly hard on Pietro during this project.

The Windber community also experienced some not-welcomed changes during this time with several groups of Italian immigrants forming the local Italian mafia.

One day when Pietro was working with Justino they showed up at the D'Arcangelo family home asking to speak with Justino.

"Pietro, where is your father?" asked one of the men.

"I'm here," said Justino. "Pietro, Alfred, and John go into the house."

Pietro and his brothers went into the home and peered out the holes that were soon going to be windows.

"I want to offer your family protection," said the man to Justino. "It's going to cost you, but not as much as it's costing everyone else. What do you think."

"Let me go get the money," said Justino.

Justino came into the house and reached for his old rusted red metal toolbox and took out the top. Inside was a gun. He quickly loaded it with bullets and went back outside.

"Papa," said Pietro.

"Stay put," said Justino.

Pietro and his brothers peered out the window as Justino went back outside to speak with the men. He held the gun up.

"If you ever show back on my property, you won't leave alive," said Justino. "Now get the hell out of here."

The men backed up abruptly and left. Justino waited several minutes, standing outside, gun in hand.

Weeks later rumors of the mafia were still running through the Windber community. The word was that the Italian mafia hated Lorenzo. One night late, he was jumped by the group and killed.

From that point forward the mafia faded away in Windber and the town became safer.

Pietro and Justino spent their days in the mines and their nights and weekends continuing to work on the house with Alfred and John.

Despite the fact that Justino was angry and tough on him during the project, Pietro admired his persistence. The love for his father grew as he watched him accomplish his life-long goal of building and owning a family home.

After two years of grueling work, the house was complete.

Very soon afterward, Pietro wed Nicolette on a sunny Saturday in May. The D'Arcangelo and Di Loreto families and their friends celebrated the marriage at Saint Anthony's of Padua in Windber. A traditional Roman Catholic Italian wedding, the priest conducted the ceremony with a reception at the church following.

Anna and Nicolette's mother made every Italian cookie imaginable from vanilla and anise pizzelles to Italian butter cookies. The cookies were lined beautifully around the cake on the dessert table. Pietro and Nicolette and their friends and family danced the tarantella late into the evening. Family and

A STORY ABOUT PIZZA

friends ate homemade bread, pasta and meatballs, with all the food made by the D'Arcangelo and Di Loreto families for the ceremony. Pietro and Nicolette lovingly drove off after the ceremony eager to start their new life together.

After the wedding, Nicolette moved into the D'Arcangelo family home with Pietro.

During that time life seemed to stand still. But sometimes when life stands still it's preparing you for your next battle.

Chapter 7 Recipe
Wedding Cookies

(Italian Butter Cookies)

Ingredients

16 eggs

3 tablespoons vanilla

1 lb of butter

3 cups of sugar

3 tablespoons baking powder

12-13 cups of Flour

Icing Ingredients

4 cups of powdered sugar

2 teaspoon vanilla

8 tablespoons of milk

Optional: Sprinkles (round rainbow or white)

Directions:

Separate eggs into two bowls. Add sugar and vanilla to yolks, Beat in whites and add to mixture.

Then add your dry ingredients slowly. Mix until you get your cookie batter.

Scoop round cookies onto a greased cookie sheet, or use parchment paper. Bake at 350 degrees for 12 minutes.

A STORY ABOUT PIZZA

For the icing, add the powdered sugar, vanilla, and milk until you get a medium-thick glaze. Dip cool cookies into the glaze then add the sprinkles on top.

Chapter 8
Justino D'Arcangelo

As days turned into months, then years, Justino aged.

From the years of hard physical labor in the mines, his health deteriorated. Nevertheless, he spent his days in the mines and nights still finalizing details on his family home.

Days after the exterior of the home was done Pietro heard men yelling in the mine.

"Help, get an ambulance," yelled one of the miners. "He's not breathing."

Pietro feared an accident but what he saw was much worse. Justino emerged and was being carried out by three fellow miners. He had collapsed and was having trouble breathing.

"Papa," said Pietro as he grabbed Justino's hand. "Just try to breathe."

Pietro rushed his father to the local miner's hospital praying the entire way there. As they arrived Justino's breathing was labored and he was in and out of consciousness. The doctor saw him and gave him some morphine to calm him down. As he lay peacefully in the bed, the doctor and nurse told Pietro it didn't look good.

Justino's lungs were deteriorating from black lung and he was losing his ability to breathe.

Pietro sat by his father's side holding his hand. As he looked at him he saw the wrinkles in Justino's face, his white hair. He felt the roughness of his hand and saw his worn body.

A STORY ABOUT PIZZA

"Papa," he said. "It's ok. Everything is going to be ok."

At that moment, Pietro really saw Justino for the first time. A strong man, hard working, a provider. Loyal to the core and loving his wife and family.

He was also complicated, worn and had his flaws. No matter what happened he kept on going, working, fighting for their family.

For the first time in his life, when Pietro looked at Justino he didn't see his resentful father stomping off to work, short tempered and tired. He saw Justino for who he was. He saw the love that Justino had for him, his mother, and his brothers and how life had beaten him down even though he spent so long fighting.

Justino looked up at Pietro at that moment and said in Italian, "Non l'ho mai detto ma sono sempre stato fiero di te. Ti voglio bene figlio mio."

"I have never said it, but I have always been proud of you. I love you, my son."

Pietro sobbed as Justino passed away in the hospital that day. His heart was broken. Pietro loved his father unconditionally, despite his faults, as his father loved him, his mother, and his brothers.

At that moment Pietro realized that to truly love someone, is to also love their flaws.

Growing up, Pietro felt he had so many reasons to hate his father. He silently held that resentment as a young boy, but could finally let it go.

A wise man once said, to love, for all the reasons you should not, is greatness. Pietro knew that because of Justino he had become a hard-working, loyal man. As his life ended in that moment Pietro let go. It would be impossible to imagine a life without his father in it.

Over the next week, the D'Arcangelo family laid Justino to rest. Anna, Alfred, and John were joined by Justino's brother Angelo and Angelo's wife Maria from New York. Domenick returned briefly from the service to mourn his father.

All of the Berwind miners attended Justino's funeral and celebrated his life.

Because of Justino's work with Berwind-White Coal Company over the years, Anna was awarded his benefits.

The boys and Anna were living in one part of the newly built family home, while Pietro and Nicolette moved into the other side of the home that was unfinished.

Domenick returned to the service. Alfred and John were now contemplating their own futures. Alfred wanted to become a bricklayer. John was planning to go into the military.

Pietro would spend the next few months helping his family grieve over the loss of Justino and he would forever remember the life of his father.

Chapter 8 Recipe
Italian Braciole Sauce Recipe

Ingredients

2 pound flank steak

2 10 oz cans of tomato sauce

1 4 oz can of tomato paste

4 tablespoons of olive oil

6 cloves of garlic

1 cup of bread crumbs

1 cup parmesan cheese

1 tablespoon of salt

1 teaspoon of pepper

Directions:

Mix the parmesan cheese, 2 cloves of garlic (diced), bread crumbs, and 2 tablespoons of olive oil in a bowl. Pound the flank steak until it's ¼ inch thick then cut into strips. Add the mixture from the bowl to the flank steak and roll each strip. Wrap each piece with twine.

Add diced garlic and olive oil to a large pan and put on medium heat. Drop in the flank steak rolls and cook on each side, about 5-6 minutes each.

In a large pot add two more cloves of garlic and olive oil. Cook on medium until oil bubbles and garlic starts to lightly brown. Add the tomato paste and fry for several minutes. Then add each can of sauce. Rinse the can with water (about half way) and add the water. Bring the sauce to a boil and stir then put on low.

Gently drop the Braciole into the sauce and cook the sauce on low with the meat. When serving, remove the twine from the meat before eating.

Chapter 9
The Berwind-White Coal Company

The Berwind-White Coal Mines were in operation well before the D'Arcangelo family traveled to America from Italy. In fact Berwind-White began its operations in 1886 and ended up being a leading coal distributor in the United States. They opened Mine 30 in 1897 followed by Mines 31 and 32. Eventually they became a commercial business center in the town of Windber.

Berwind-White owned thirteen different mining locations in the area with three in Windber where Pietro and the D'Arcangelo family lived for many years.

In addition to the mines' company homes that housed the D'Arcangelo's and other miners' families, other buildings were constructed as well: a hospital, bank, Eureka store which was the Berwind-White Coal Company Store, and many historic buildings that are still intact today.

By the late 1950s many miners had fallen victim to black lung. There were also a series of mining accidents and disasters. In fact, between the years of 1897 to 1962, 343 miners lost their lives in Berwind-White mines in Windber alone.

Pietro, since his first day working in the mines as a boy, knew he needed to change the course for himself.

Still grieving from the loss of his father, Justino, Pietro was now married and the head of his own family. He was even more determined to create his own path in life.

Pietro had spent years saving money and purchased a white Rambler Nash that he used to help haul coal from the back. From all the years of his hard work, this was one of the first things he ever bought for himself.

One day, as Pietro pulled up to the mines to pick up a batch of coal, he saw the miners all standing around outside. He parked his Nash near the loading area and got out of the car. Pietro noticed pink slips in many of the miner's hands. When he looked up at their stained black dirty faces, he noticed a range of emotions on their faces. Some of the miners had single tears streaming down their eyes. Others were smiling and toasting with bottles of beer. There were also the old folks; the senior minors who sat down for what seemed like the first time since working in the mines. They carried looks of disbelief.

The local Windber mines owned by Berwind-White Coal Company were closing.

As Pietro walked through the crowd, he saw his supervisor. As they made their way to each other in what seemed like slow motion, he handed Pietro the pink piece of paper. As Pietro held that pink piece of paper in his rough hand, tears filled his eyes. The mines had been the reason his family came to America. They made up his father's entire career. He had worked there most of his life and he knew he had dreaded every moment. For the first time, he just felt one thing. Relief.

A STORY ABOUT PIZZA

But for Pietro, the end of his work in the mines was bittersweet. He was now faced with the challenge of how he would take care of his family. A worry that many of the miners now had.

Nicolette was pregnant with their first child and Pietro had been struggling with his own health issues from being injured in the mines and black lung. As he made his way home with his Rambler Nash filled with what coal was left he knew he had to talk with Nicolette.

Pietro pulled up to the house, took his pink slip from the passenger side and walked into the house. Pregnant, Nicolette was making trays of chicken cutlets and meatballs in preparation for the baby, so the family would have food.

She looked up and immediately knew what this meant. With tears in her eyes she waddled over to Pietro and the two hugged. "Que Sa Ra Sa Ra," she said. "Whatever will be will be."

Thankfully, it would be a few weeks before the mines closed for good and Pietro found out in the coming days that he was eligible for some benefits for his years of service. Even though it was very small it was something.

Pietro still had very big dreams and wasn't about to let them go. Now was the time to take action and work on creating the next phase of his life. He prayed that night and asked God to help him to be strong. He asked for courage so he could build the life of his family that he always dreamed of.

Chapter 9 Recipe
Meatballs

Ingredients

1 lb ground beef

1 lb ground pork

2 eggs

¼ cup fresh parsley

1 tablespoon salt

1 tablespoon fresh garlic

2 tablespoons fresh basil

1 teaspoon black pepper

1 ½ cups breadcrumbs

½ cup parmesan cheese

1 teaspoon olive oil

Directions:

Mix the meat and eggs together in a mixer or by hand. Add in the breadcrumbs and cheese and then the spices. Mix well. Roll the meat into golf ball sized balls.

Use the olive oil to grease two making sheets. Add the meatballs there about a half an inch apart (this recipe should make two pans). Bake at 375 degrees for 15 mins then flip them and bake for another 15 minutes.

Once they're done place them in a colander with a paper towel. Then add them to tomato sauce, or bag and freeze.

A STORY ABOUT PIZZA

Chapter 10
D'Arc's Market

It was Saturday and time for Pietro to think about what he was going to do next. Going for a walk always helped him give him perspective and the ability to figure out a solution to his problems.

As he walked past a local restaurant called The Fairway, he noted a building and parking lot owned by the Rillow family. Pietro thought back to when he was a boy and how much he loved the market, the food, and the vendors.

At that moment Pietro had an idea. He could set up a market just like the ones he loved from his childhood.

Pietro spoke with the Rillow family about using the space for an initial outdoor setup. The market would be run by Pietro. Nicolette and his mother, Anna, would help.

They would sell basic food items, baked goods, and in-season produce.

Pietro knew a local supplier and was able to get some soups and, of course, pasta. Anna and Nicolette baked some Italian desserts and breads.

Western Pennsylvania had an ample produce supply from the families' local gardens so this would be plentiful during the summer and early fall.

During the days, Nicolette and Anna ran the market while Pietro was finishing his final months working in the mines. Pietro would spend the entire day working in the mine and then work at the market in the evenings.

Because the market was outside, Anna and Nicolette loved it during the spring, summer, and fall. Everyone struggled during the winter months. Nicolette would walk to the market and home daily as would Anna. They often encountered high winds, snow, and below-freezing temperatures closing the market many days. The lack of seasonal produce and transportation for supplies was also a problem when the weather was poor.

However, even with all of the problems, the D'Arcangelo family managed to get through their first year running the market. To compensate for the lack of produce sales, Nicolette and Anna would make pizza frittas; fried dough with sugar. They were a local favorite, the aroma filling the kitchen the night before the market as they came out of the oven piping hot.

As the spring flowers started to bloom and the rains faded, the best time of the year was about to begin. Summer.

The market was bustling, the produce was plentiful, and the nights were cool and breezy. Walking to and from the market was no problem at all and at the end of the evening they could smell the crisp air and neighbors cooking dinner as Pietro, Nicolette, and Anna made their way home.

Best of all, the summer produce in Western, Pennsylvania was plentiful.

Summer seemed to fly by. As June quickly turned into August there was also something else on the way. Nicolette was very pregnant. On a hot day at the end of August she gave birth to a daughter, who they called Linda.

Now, with a baby in hand, it would be challenging for Nicolette to run the outdoor market. It was time for the

D'Arcangelo family to take their next step: finding a real location to run their market indoors.

Pietro had seen a building just down the street that was for sale. It belonged to Berwind-White Coal Company and was a Eureka Hardware store. He looked at the building constructed of light yellow Windber brick with windows in front. This was it.

Now Pietro wasn't just slowly walking. He was racing home to count his money; money he had saved for many, many years of hard physical labor in the coal mines since he was a boy. After counting his money, he prayed and prayed. He prayed for the rest of the day and at mass that Sunday.

At 8:00 a.m. on Monday morning, he took every cent he had, and drove down to the bank to make a down payment on the building at 2013 Graham Avenue. As he counted the dollars and cents, his hands shook with excitement. Pietro felt like he was dreaming as this had been his dream for his entire life, since he was a boy. He had pictured it in his mind over and over again. Now it was finally happening.

When Pietro walked into the bank, he was greeted at once by Mr. Russo. His father had worked with Justino in the mines and Pietro knew him from school.

"Hello, Mr. Russo, nice to see you again," said Pietro. "I want to buy the yellow brick building on 2013 Graham Avenue."

"Hello, Pietro," said Mr. Russo. "Ok, let's fill out some paperwork. What do you have in terms of money saved for the building?"

"I have a down payment of $727.00 on the building," said Pietro.

"Ok," said Mr. Russo. "The total cost of the building is $35,000.00. I assume you'll need a loan for the rest of the money. Would you like to see the building?"

"No," said Pietro. "Let's sign the papers."

As he proudly left the bank, Pietro couldn't wait to get home to Nicolette and his mother.

After a few weeks of preparation, more paperwork and more prayers, Pietro got the keys to the building.

As he turned the key, Pietro's hands were shaking. He was about to walk into his new building. The door creaked as Pietro looked inside. Nicolette and Anna were right behind him with all of their cleaning supplies.

It was dark and the windows were dirty. With the little bit of light that showed in, Pietro looked around slowly. He saw wood floors stained black, and 18-foot high ornamental ceilings. Dusty shelves were sitting up throughout the floor. They would be perfect for canned and boxed goods.

"It's beautiful," said Anna. "I love it."

"It's perfect," Nicolette agreed. "Look at the size of the main level. We can put a kitchen here in the back and have the store here and supplies on this shelf and food on these," pointing to the different locations in the room excitedly.

On the second floor were two apartments that would need to be fixed up. The basement had a coal furnace where Pietro could heat the entire building.

A STORY ABOUT PIZZA

The building, dirty and in need of some work, was exactly what he was looking for. Pietro already had the tools and supplies from the home that he built with his father several years before. He would take them from the basement storage of the house and start his work on the building right away.

Despite any work that needed to be done, Pietro thought it was a beautiful building. This was the building that he had always dreamed of. He and his family would need to get it cleaned, painted and set up so he could open for business. Most importantly, Pietro was finally home.

Anna and Nicolette got right to work. They would make it spotless.

Pietro would build and set up his store with an entrance so they could open as soon as possible. Then he would fix up the upstairs apartment for his family to move into eventually. He would rent out the family home he had built with Justino.

During the next few weeks Pietro worked day and night to get the store ready. While he was building shelves and setting it up, Nicolette was finding food and supplies to order to stock the shelves.

D'Arcangelo's Store sold all the necessary food items for local families, everything from meat, homemade sausage, Stein Kersheners food items.

The shelf behind the counters also had tomato paste, sauce puree, and a rack with pasta from Cumberland Macaroni. There were even shelves to the ceiling with a ladder that connected to the ceiling. When the ladder was pushed the shelves displayed could see Corelle dishes and pasta makers. Low shelves were full of kidney beans, pork and beans, and

Campbell's soup. And, of course there were two glass cases with cheese and meat with a meat slicer.

Miner families and other locals from the Windber community would go there and shop every Saturday. Nicolette had even set up charge accounts for local customers.

LaMonica's, owned by a friend of the D'Arcangelo family, had a bakery and delivered homemade Italian bread and buns to the store. Pietro even brought in his favorite varieties of ice cream from Fairview Dairy just up the street as he loved ice cream almost as much as he loved pizza.

Over the following months D'Arcangelo's Market became a family landmark for the Windber community and everyone knew Pietro from Berwind-White Coal Company.

While the store was bustling, Pietro decided to get the apartments renovated. One of them would be the new D'Arcangelo family home where Pietro, Nicolette, Linda, and Anna would live.

As Pietro was working one day, a local woman named Pearl Leonardis came into the store. Pearl was a local widow. She was kind and cheerful, never argumentative.

Despite the fact that Pearl had lost her husband many years earlier, she had a positive outlook on life. She decided to give her family home, a white house located behind Windber Builders, to her daughter and son-in-law and her grandchildren. Pearl needed a small place and she had heard that Pietro might have an apartment for rent.

Pietro would need a few months to have the other apartment ready but that day, he and Pearl made an agreement that she would be his very first tenant. Pearl walked home

A STORY ABOUT PIZZA

feeling hopeful and excited to start a new chapter. Little did she know she would be much more than a tenant to the D'Arcangelo family.

Chapter 10 Recipe
Pizza Frittas

Ingredients

5 cups of white flour

2 packs of fast-rise yeast

1 tablespoon salt (or a pinch)

1 tablespoon of white sugar

2 cups of warm water

Half a cup of cooking oil (olive oil)

Topping

1 cup white sugar to sprinkle on top

Optional: Add raisins

Directions:

In a mixer or a bowl add in the dry ingredients starting with the flour. Make a hole in the middle of the bowl and add the yeast, salt and sugar. Start slowly adding the water as you mix the dough until you get a nice consistency.

Cover the let dough rise for an hour. Cut pieces from the dough and form them on a lightly greased cookie sheet. Nicolette and Anna created an elongated shape for their pizza frittas. Lay them out on the sheet and cover. Let rise for about 20 minutes.

Add oil to a pan and turn the heat to medium. Test the oil by dropping in a tiny bit of water and seeing if it bubbles. Add

A STORY ABOUT PIZZA

in the first fritta, flip after a few minutes and cook until lightly golden brown.

Remove from oil and lay on a plate on a paper towel to get rid of excess oil. Lightly dust with white sugar.

Chapter 11
D'Arc's Pizza

After months of hard work, Pietro had done it. He renovated both upstairs apartments at D'Arcangelo's Store. His family was moving out of their home on 22nd Street and into the building on Graham Avenue in Windber.

His first tenant, Pearl, was also moving into her apartment with the help of her family.

D'Arcangelo's Market was growing. Everyone in town now knew about it, and shopped there. Nicolette, now pregnant with her second child, ran the store with Pietro's mother Anna. They made sure that the orders were made to the vendors, kept track of the charge accounts, cleaned, and talked with the local customers who had now become friends. Pearl was also helping in the market and had grown quite close to the family in the short time she lived at 2013 Graham Avenue.

In her spare time Anna helped cook and clean. She was always busy making sure dinner was on the stove, with the market busier than ever. Pietro would walk to the upstairs apartment smelling Anna's homemade polenta or whatever Italian delicacy she decided to make that day.

Pietro and Nicolette were good business partners. Pietro made sure the building was running and the store was stocked, and Nicolette kept track of the books, supplies, and merchant and customer accounts. However, as well as Pietro and Nicolette worked together, they argued just as much.

Nicolette had a strong personality and Pietro felt she should be submissive in the marriage. Pietro's mother had

A STORY ABOUT PIZZA

always listened to Justino, and was careful not to argue or upset him. Although he could never treat Nicolette the way that his father treated his mother, he did expect his wife to remain confined to the traditional role of a wife. However, Nicolette had other ideas, even insisting on working when Pietro specifically told her not to.

One day, Nicolette was stocking the shelves at the market as it had been an unusually busy day. As Pietro walked in he told her to stop.

"What do you mean stop?" said Nicolette. "We're out of almost everything and I have to keep the shelves stocked."

"That's a man's job," said Pietro. "Women can't do that job right."

"Pete," said Nicolette, as this is often what she called him especially when she was upset with him. "Goddammit, Pete, how dare you speak to me like that. I hope you drop dead on the spot," said Nicolette.

"Shut the hell up, Nicolette," Pietro said. He stomped off and went for a walk.

While Pietro and Nicolette often had these bickering types of arguments, both were quick to forgive. Pietro thought about his parents as he walked down the street. He had a hard time stepping out of the beliefs he was raised into. He didn't want his wife to work, or even to have an opinion. But, he needed her to work with him at the same time.

Just down the street, the D'Arcangelo's good friend Rhoda Leone and her husband Erino also owned a market where they made submarine sandwiches.

ERICA D'ARCANGELO

Everyone called Erino Harry. The D'Arcangelo's often ordered sandwiches from there, served on LaMonica's buns. The same buns were sold at D'Arcangelo's Market. Pietro would go pick them up and chat about business, working in the mines, and how Windber had grown over the last few years.

Just up the street, the Rillow family still had a restaurant. They also had opened a meat market and a tavern. The tavern later became one of the first full-menu Italian restaurants in Windber when their daughter Mildred Rillow married Anthony Rizzo. Rizzo's Restaurant served homemade authentic Italian food, pasta dishes, and desserts.

The east end of Windber had grown into a strong Italian community and businesses were thriving. In the west end of Windber lived many Polish, Irish, and Slovakian Immigrants. The entire community was a melting pot of different ethnicities forming the Windber Community.

Many of them were former coal miners now opening new businesses in this small town in western Pennsylvania. Times were changing and Pietro decided he was willing to change in his own way.

He was very well-known in Windber from his days of working in the mines with his father. He often stopped at the local store and talked with his friends and other business owners.

Even though D'Arcangelo's Market was thriving, Pietro was always thinking of his next steps. He wanted to grow his business and leave a legacy for his children.

He walked down the street in Windber, he stopped to get some supplies for the store for Anna and Nicolette. After

A STORY ABOUT PIZZA

grabbing some milk and eggs he saw some pizza for sale near the cash register. Pietro thought this pizza looked completely different from the pizza he had in Italy. The slices he still dreamed about, even as a grown man.

They were thick, cold slices, wrapped in plastic. He picked one slice of pizza up, and turned it over. Four cents. Pietro decided to buy the pizza and try it out.

As he walked home he took the pizza out of the plastic wrapper and ate it.

It was terrible. Since it was a sin to throw away food, Pietro finished the slice. But during his last bite something came to him.

While D'Arcangelo's Market had taken off there was something more on the horizon. Seeing the community of Windber flourish after the mines closed was something Pietro had dreamt about since he was a boy. But there was one dream that he never forgot about.

His very first love: pizza.

He thought about this over the next few days but said nothing as Pietro often needed time to think about his next steps before saying anything out loud to anyone, even to Nicolette and Anna.

In the back corner of the market sat an old gas stove. Nicolette and Anna used it to bake Easter bread in the spring and other small items to sell in the store, like Italian bread, and pizza frittas, fried dough with sugar and raisins.

Pietro looked at it every time he walked into the store as it reminded him of the old Italian stoves that were used to make pizza in Italy when he was a boy.

One day, while looking at the old gas stove, Pete said, "Nicolette, we need more customers in the market. How do we get more people in here?"

Nicolette, in a sarcastic sharp-witted tone replied, "I don't know Pete. You're the man. Women can't think of these complex ideas according to you."

To which Pietro replied, "Goddammit, Nicolette." He slammed down a tool he was holding.

Pearl was standing nearby listening to the conversation, one she had heard many times. Usually she stayed quiet, chuckling to herself, during these discussions. However, this time she answered.

"We should sell pizza here," she said cheerfully but quietly.

Pietro and Nicolette both perked up.

"Yes we should," said Pietro.

This was music to Pietro's ears. He and Nicolette looked around their store to see if they had the necessary items to make pizza. Nicolette found some rectangular metal cooking sheets. Those would work perfectly. She opened up two of them and promptly washed and tried them.

Pietro found a bag of flour and some yeast. Using a large metal mixing bowl, he mixed them together and added some warm water, a pinch of salt and sugar, and mixed his first batch of dough. After the dough was mixed he laid a kitchen towel on top of it to let it rise.

He would need to figure out the cheese and sauce.

A STORY ABOUT PIZZA

As Pietro gazed around the store, he saw the Red Pack tomato paste and sauce cans and opened them up. He then found some spices that Anna used and mixed those up: parsley, basil, oregano, onion powder and garlic, as well as salt and pepper. After Pietro got the sauce mixed he turned around to see that Nicolette had found him the cheese for the trays: a very nice mozzarella and a white American cheese with a little bit of Parmesan.

Pietro cleaned the counter, washing and drying it thoroughly. He spread some flour on it and rolled out his dough that had raised beautifully. From this batch Pietro got two very nice trays of pizza.

Using the imported Italian olive oil from the store he greased the pans. He carefully moved the dough from the counter to the pans, gently pushing the edges against the edge of the sheet pan. Pietro spread the sauce on each pizza, lightly. He added the parmesan and the American cheese and topped the pizza with mozzarella.

Both of the pizzas went into the oven. Pietro checked on them every few minutes flipping them around to make sure both sides were evenly cooked. When he saw the cheese turn light brown and start to bubble he took the pizzas out of the oven and put them on the counter.

While the pizzas were cooking, Anna smelled them and came into the kitchen area.

Now Anna, Nicolette, Pearl and Pietro were ready to try the slices.

Thankfully, Nicolette had found a pizza cutter in the store that they used to cut their first tray of pizza.

As all four of them took their first bites of pizza, they were completely silent.

For Pietro, it took him back to being a child, where he sat outside the pizzeria eating a fresh slice of pizza without a care in the world. At that point Pietro, Anna, Nicolette, and Pearl all agreed that D'Arc's would start selling pizza.

"This is delicious," said Pearl.

"The best pizza I've ever had," replied Anna.

"Nicolette?" said Pietro.

"Pretty good for a man," she replied.

Everyone chuckled.

It was settled. D'Arcangelo's Market would sell pizza.

Over the next few days they all prepared. Anna, Nicolette, and Pearl got even more pans ready. They created a space in front of the oven to make the dough as well as a sauce and cheese station. Nicolette made a large container of sauce. Pearl hand grated, packaged, and refrigerated all the cheese.

While they did that Pietro showed them how he made the dough and they started making even bigger batches.

Now was the time for Pietro to get the word out about the pizza. He had Nicolette draw a sign for D'Arc's Pizza with days and hours that they would have it available.

For now, they would serve it on plates, napkins, or paper towels but Pietro had just ordered pizza boxes which would arrive in a few weeks. The pizza could go into an open-faced box for those that wanted to eat it there. Each box could hold

A STORY ABOUT PIZZA

about 9 pieces. A second box could be used as a lid, and two boxes of pizza would be a tray with fifteen slices total.

The local post office had a mimeograph machine and Pietro's friend worked there. He took the sign in and got ten copies of it to advertise the pizza.

Pietro went to Berwind-White Coal Company where they still maintained their business office and asked permission to hang up the sign. Everyone there knew Pietro and Justino so, of course, he was given permission to do so.

Pietro also went to Bestform Sewing Factory, the new Eureka Store that relocated just up the street, and the local hospital. That Thursday would be the first day that D'Arc's would be offering pizza at their market.

Over the next few days, the store was the busiest it had ever been. Customers and friends from all across town had stopped in to the market to ask about the pizza.

Anna and Pearl were running around like crazy. Nicolette, who was about to give birth to her second child, couldn't move around as much but was working to keep the records on the charge accounts in order and make sure the pricing was set up for the pizza which they would sell for five cents per slice.

Pietro had even ordered pepperoni from his butcher friend who provided meat for the store. One tray of pizza would be fifteen slices, and customers could choose a plain slice of pepperoni. Pietro decided to add the pepperoni after it was cooked to make sure nothing was wasted in case the customers liked the plain slices better.

Before any of them knew it, it was Thursday. Pietro, Nicolette, Pearl, and Anna all got to work early. While Italian music played throughout the store they all prepared the pizza ingredients, rolled the dough, sauced and cheesed pizzas, and preheated the oven.

Nicolette would sit at the front and ring up customers. Pietro would be in charge of cooking. Anna and Pearl would prepare the pizzas and handle the dishes. Even Linda was there running around sampling the pizzas.

When Pietro walked over to open the market he couldn't believe his eyes. All of his friends from Windber showed up to support him. The line for D'Arc's Pizza was all the way down the street.

For a moment Pietro stopped. His eyes welled up with tears. His entire life flashed before his eyes. Growing up with his parents and brothers, working in the coal mines.

How every day he had prayed for a new life. A life he dreamt about and now a life that he had finally created. In this brief moment Pietro was truly happy to serve the people he loved, in the community he called home.

As he opened the doors, the community poured in. He watched the proud and happy looks on his mother's, wife's, and friends' faces as they saw how many people showed up for the pizza.

The D'Arcangelo's served pizza that day until 9:00 p.m. when they had fully run out of all the ingredients and were exhausted. They would have pizza again the next day as well as the weekend. Pietro had already ordered more supplies that would be delivered in the morning.

A STORY ABOUT PIZZA

They cleaned up and closed for the night. Second only to his wedding and the birth of his daughter, it was the very best night of Pietro's life.

Chapter 11 Recipe
Anna's Polenta

Ingredients

1 cup instant mashed potatoes

2 teaspoons of salt

6 ¼ cup boiling water

2 ½ cups of cornmeal

2 cups of cold water

Directions:

Bring 6 cups of water to a boil and add salt. Mix in ½ cup of cornmeal with 1 cup of mashed potatoes. Reduce heat to simmer and slowly add the additional 2 cups of cornmeal mixture stirring constantly with a whisk until the polenta has been fully incorporated.

Grate parmesan reggiano on the top.

We recommend adding a veggie sauce as well cooked with some loose Italian sausage.

Chapter 12
The Shop + The Pizza Oven

As a day turned into a week, it became a month, and then a year. Nicolette had given birth to the D'Arcangelo's second child, a son, Emery. She was resting upstairs with the new baby, keeping busy with the store books, and paperwork, as well as cooking for the family, and keeping the house up.

Downstairs, D'Arc's Market was bustling with customers who couldn't get enough of the pizza. Pietro had hired Nicolette's sister Rose and her brother Pundy to help work at the shop while Anna managed the store. Pearl helped Anna with the store and with the pizza shop as well.

Pietro was a busy man. But the more productive and busy a man is, the happier he is.

He now had two small children, and a successful business to run. It was not without its challenges, but Pietro was truly happy. After facing a lifetime of struggle he understood that no success is without struggle, and was willing to face these head on.

Even though D'Arc's Pizza was busy, Pietro always feared down times. He made sure that he was active in the community, having Nicolette call all of the businesses to let them know there would be pizza available and taking orders.

Thankfully the D'Arcangelo's had many close friends and were well-known in Windber from working in the mines. There, Pietro got a lot of support.

Pietro also saved his money. He remembered the days when his family didn't have anything and lived in fear of losing what they had.

Pietro's brother Alfred had also decided to live in Windber and was a bricklayer. He helped Pietro maintain the building and do some brickwork outside. The building had been built in 1905 and was often in need of upkeep and repair. Pietro spent a lot of his time maintaining this as well.

Sleep was something that was scarce to Pietro. He was up all throughout the night with Nicolette and the children as well as making his rounds around the building to make sure that everything was in working order. It would be winter again in just a few months and he would need to make sure the coal furnace could adequately heat the building and that the exterior didn't have any holes.

However, for the first time in a long time, due to how careful he was, Pietro and Nicolette had been able to save some money. They decided to buy some materials and a pizza oven to expand D'Arc's Pizza. Over the next few months Pietro added a renovation project to his busy schedule. He was able to get some help with this one by hiring some of his friends from the mines who helped to fix up houses.

D'Arc's expanded the kitchen area with a bigger oven. Pietro's brother drove with him two hours north, near Pittsburgh, to pick up the new pizza oven. They could barely fit the oven into the back of Pietro's Rambler. They then drove back and installed it that day.

Where the gas stove could only cook two trays at once, this oven could cook at least four at a time, doubling the amount of pizza that Pietro could make. This was an advantage as they had been selling out most nights.

Along with the oven, Pietro purchased additional refrigerators and freezers as well as shelves for supplies, and pizza boxes. He also moved the space around and separated the pizza area from the market itself so the shop would allow for even more customers.

Pietro found some old tables and had them delivered. He set them up with chairs so people could sit down and enjoy their pizza when they came into D'Arcangelo's Market, and catch up with friends.

The market became full of friends and family, sitting and chatting while they enjoyed a few slices. Anna and Nicolette often made pizza frittas and pizzelles and Pearl would put on a pot of coffee.

The women would sit and fold pizza boxes, chatting and laughing together about the day or the challenges of the business.

On Sundays the market and shop were closed. The D'Arcangelo family went to mass at St. Anthony's of Padua Church that was right up the street.

After church they cooked a traditional Italian lunch including some pasta, meatballs, chicken cutlets, and of course, desserts and coffee.

Often, Nicolette's and Pietro's families would join them. They sat at a big table in the upstairs dining room, laughing and drinking red wine. After lunch aunts, uncles, and cousins would take a siesta (nap) with people sleeping on couches and floors throughout the D'Arcangelo home.

After this day of relaxation, Pietro, Nicolette, Anna, and Pearl would prepare for the Monday deliveries at the market which was open six days a week. The D'Arcangelo's sold pizza on Thursday through Saturday.

Chapter 12 Recipe
Ravioli's

Ingredients

1 egg

1 cup of flour

1 tablespoon of sour cream

½ cup warm water

1 large container of ricotta cheese

½ cup of parmesan cheese

1 tablespoon of fresh parsley

1 tablespoon of fresh basil

1 teaspoon of salt

1 teaspoon of pepper

Directions:

Mix one egg, flour, sour cream and warm water in a mixer or bowl. Lightly knead. Set aside. You can double the ingredients and mix two batches of dough but mix them separately.

Mix ricotta cheese, parmesan, parsley, basil, salt and pepper. Set aside.

Roll out the dough so it is 1/16th thick. Cut the dough into strips and drop a tablespoon of the mixture onto the beginning of the strip leaving about a 1/16th of an inch of space. Cut dough to fold over and use a fork or a ravioli maker to close the ravioli. Do this until all the ravioli's are made.

Get a large pot of salted boiling water ready. Gently drop ravioli into the pot and cook for 3-4 minutes until they float to the top. Serve with your favorite sauce.

Chapter 13
Family

Very early on, Pietro had learned that nothing was more important than family. He and Nicolette now had two children: Linda Emery. They would run and play around the pizza shop while the family worked, laughing while eating whatever Italian delicacy that Nicolette, Pietro, or Anna made that day.

The store was stocked with food and supplies, and busy with family members coming in and out. D'Arc's Pizza had added a few additional toppings to their menu other than the original plain and pepperoni slices.

Nicolette and her sister Rose started making homemade meatballs that Pietro used to eat on LaMonica's rolls. Pietro also had a large skillet on the gas stove with hot sausage, peppers, and onions that the family would snack on throughout the day. The local produce, grown by the family, and harvested in the summer and fall would be enough to supply the onions and peppers for the food.

Soon enough D'Arc's Pizza started selling both meatball and hot sausage sandwiches for a quarter each, ten cents with cheese. The D'Arcangelo children would run in and out of the shop, grabbing a slice of pizza from the cutting board or making a quick sandwich as they greeted everyone in the store.

Even though Emery was only a few feet tall at the time, he loved basketball. During the warm months he played a block down from the D'Arcangelo building at East End School District until after dark. Nicolette would yell his name at dinner time and he would come running up the sidewalk with his basketball in hand.

During the winter, Pietro put an indoor hoop up for Emery in the back storage room where supply coolers were stacked against the far wall. The coolers not only contained pizza toppings, but gallon-sized vats of ice cream. Pietro's favorite flavor was chocolate marshmallow, but he also loved butter pecan. Of course, he had to have some rainbow ice cream for his kids.

Pietro was a kind and caring father. He often took Linda and Emery with him to get supplies for the store and pizza shop. But his days and nights were filled with work, which he happily did to take care of his family.

Nicolette handled the books, kept track of the charge accounts, and was the "mother" of the shop, often giving unsolicited and frank advice to family members.

Though Pietro was careful and conservative, he had a love of something other than pizza and his family. This love was for cars. He had sold his white Rambler Nash and purchased a burnt-orange Chevy pickup truck to haul pizza and store supplies that could not be delivered. He also picked up a 1970 Cadillac DeVille.

On a rainy Saturday morning Pietro took Emery to one of his favorite places to look for new products for the store. It was the Italian market in Pittsburgh called The Strip District. The district was named as it was a narrow strip of land that ran along the Allegheny River.

"Emerico, wake up," said Pietro. "We're going somewhere special today."

"What time is it?" Emerico asked as he sat up and rubbed his eyes.

A STORY ABOUT PIZZA

"It's early," said Pietro. "Still dark but we need to make it there in time to enjoy the day."

Pietro hadn't been there since he was a boy and went on the train with his mother, father, and two brothers. At that time the Strip was just beginning to prosper. Today, Pietro and his son made the hour and a half drive there.

Driving into the city and parking his truck, Pietro still had the very same feeling of excitement when he went to the market. He was excited to show Emery the shops and take him to his favorite one of all; Pennsylvania Macaroni Company.

Immigrants from Italy, Germany, Poland and many other areas flocked there. Not only did they start businesses, but they provided labor to many iron mills, foundries and glass factories.

As Pietro took Emery's hand he could see the boy's eyes grow wider as he filled them with the sights, sounds, and smells of the local stores and market. The two of them walked up and down the streets sampling food while Pietro purchased some supplies for the store and pizza shop.

While there they of course had to sample the local pizza.

"Here, Emerico," said Pietro. "Take your slice. I used to have pizza just like this in Italy."

Emery smelled the pizza and took a bite.

"It's good," he said. "But not as good as our pizza."

Tired, full, and happy, Pietro and Emery made their way back to the truck to drive back to Windber. It was Saturday and D'Arc's Pizza would be opening for dinner that night. Nicolette, Anna, Pearl, and Nicolette's brother and sister would be there working. Though he would be back a little later, Pietro wanted to be there to close up and get ready for family dinner on Sunday and mass at Saint Anthony's of Padua Church.

Emery fell asleep on the drive home as Pietro sang along to some show tunes and '50s classics on the radio.

The sun started to set on the beautiful day that he had had with his son.

When Pietro got back the streets around D'Arc's Pizza were full of parked cars. He and Emery arrived back and walked in to see a line for pizza, a few locals sitting at tables eating, and their family running around saucing and cheesing trays, cooking pizzas, and doing dishes as fast as they could. Emery sat down to fold boxes with Linda while Pietro jumped in on the dishes. The family closed out that night around 10:00 p.m.

That night Pietro was exhausted. He closed the shop and unpacked the supplies he had purchased that day, gently cleaning them and putting them away. Around midnight he fell asleep on the couch. Pietro usually was up several times during the night but that night, for whatever reason, he slept deeply. He dreamt of something that he hadn't remembered since he was a boy.

In the dream it was his last day in Italy at the Italian market with his family before he immigrated to America. He remembered going to get a slice of pizza, sitting and eating it on the curb of a street and petting the local stray cat. All of the sights and sounds of the local market and, of course, his mother, father, and brothers. The dream was so vivid he felt he was there again.

A STORY ABOUT PIZZA

But, Pietro was woken up that morning by screams coming from Nicolette.

"Pete, help, Pete!," she cried.

"I'm coming, I'm coming," screamed Pietro.

He jumped up in a panic and rounded the corner of his front living room going into the hall of his home. At the front door lay his mother, Anna, collapsed in Nicolette's arms.

"Help, help," Nicolette screamed, sobbing. "She fell, Pete, she fell. She's not breathing. I don't know what to do."

Pietro ran down the hall to his mother and wife. His mother wasn't moving.

They tried to revive her, but they were unsuccessful.

"No, no," gasped Pietro, crying. "Madre!"

Anna died that morning in Nicolette's arms.

"Just when you think everything is okay, it isn't." This is how Pietro felt at the moment when he lost his mother. He felt guilt over his happiness and fear of what was to come. Her funeral, like his father's, would be another Catholic Mass.

Pietro and Nicolette, still grief-stricken, were taking care of the arrangements. They would do an open casket viewing at the local funeral home for two days for family and friends to pay their respects. On the third day, there would be a mass followed by a funeral.

Anna would be buried in the cemetery on the hill next to Justino. Nicolette had written an obituary for Anna, a loving mother and grandmother, a devoted wife,and a dedicated church, family, and community member.

Many of the families who worked with Justino and Pietro and Berwind-White Coal Company attended the viewing and funeral services. Pietro's Uncle Angelo and Aunt Maria from New York drove in to pay their respects. The service was full of family including Pietro's three brothers.

Alfred was living in Windber and attended with his wife, Isabelle. John also drove in from New York. Domenick showed up with his family in tow, having moved them to California after he got out of the service.

Pietro looked solemnly ahead as the choir sang hymns, the same hymns he had heard growing up as a child while sitting with his mother in a church pew. During mass she often was giving John and Alfred looks as they pushed each other and misbehaved. Pietro used to watch how dedicated she was when the priest gave his sermon each week. The way she showed up at mass every week on Sunday and Wednesday, no matter what. She had a true belief in the good of those around her; an unwavering faith in the people she loved.

Anna had become such a part of the family, her place interwoven within the fabrics of every person she touched, that no one ever thought she would be gone.

Pietro had always had a special bond with his mother. Her loss hit him hard, but, while he leaned on his family for support, he knew he was now the head of his family. He needed to be strong for his brothers, his wife, and most of all his children.

In the days following the burial, Pietro started to walk.

He needed time to think and get some space. He thought of his mother often and wished he had just had one more day

A STORY ABOUT PIZZA

with her. The shop felt empty without her, but Pietro knew life had to go on. He had a family of his own.

Chapter 13 Recipe
Pete's Sausage and Peppers

Ingredients

2 lbs of spicy Italian sausage (can also use sweet or a combination)

4 peppers (green, yellow, red or orange)

1 onion

2-3 garlic cloves

2-3 spicy fresh banana peppers

Fresh bread or buns

1 tablespoon of olive oil

Directions:

Add olive oil, garlic, and onion to a pan and saute on medium heat. Cut up sausage into 3 to 6-inch pieces (or buy it already cut). Add it to the pan and brown the pieces on all sides.

Cut up the peppers and add them in. Sautee. Cover and put on low.

Make a sandwich using your favorite homemade bread or bun. (Pietro used a La Monica's roll.)

Chapter 14
A Windber Tradition

Pietro would always remember his mother's kind words, especially on the day his father passed away. Although heartbroken, she was standing at the hospital with Alfred and John by her side. Pietro walked out and they embraced. She whispered into Pietro's ear and told him how much his father always loved and admired him. Anna told Pietro that day that his father's memories would never leave him. That he could look back at them any time he wanted.

Now Pietro knew that his mother's memories were there too. No matter what hardship he faced he would continue to make his family proud. Pietro would continue to serve the Windber community with the pizza shop and store and take care of his wife and children. He would honor his mother by being a good friend to everyone he met and a devout Catholic.

D'Arc's Pizza had now been in business for over ten years. Old friends and new came in for pizza and sandwiches. Emery worked at the shop in between his basketball games and practice. Linda was now in high school, and like most teenagers, had a life of her own. Nicolette and Pietro had a third son.

Friday nights in Windber were carved out for two things. In the fall, high school football. In the winter and early spring, Windber basketball. The Windber Ramblers were followed and supported by the entire community. Emery, of course, was a basketball player and a good one at that.

After games on Friday nights, D'Arc's Pizza was full of high school kids hanging out and eating pizza. The phone rang off the hook with orders from the minute they opened until 10:00 p.m. closing.

When the shop wasn't full of teenagers, the Windber community utilized the space for family dinners, reunions, or just to stop in quickly to pick up their favorite pizza or sandwich.

Between running the shop and keeping up with the building, Pietro kept himself very busy.

Saturday mornings were spent sleeping in and then waking up to the smell of coffee and pizza frittas with white sugar or raisins. Pearl was always busy next door baking pizzelle's and Italian butter cookies. The smell of anise and vanilla filled the hallway on the second floor of D'Arc's Pizza.

Sundays were of course the D'Arcangelo's only day off where they attended mass and had Sunday lunch starting with a simple salad with local lettuce, oil, and vinegar. Nicolette slow- roasted a pork chop in her sauce and always had homemade meatballs. This was accompanied by either cut mag (rigatoni), spaghetti, or homemade gnocchi.

As Emery grew older he played high school basketball. Pietro never missed a game. The D'Arc's hosted the team after every Friday night game for pizzas.

Summertime was about the same for the D'Arcangelo family. Emery had baseball practice every morning on the local courts so he could get ready for the upcoming season.

It was in the blink of an eye that both Linda and Emery went from children to teenagers. Linda finished high school and decided to settle down. She got married and was having her first child.

A STORY ABOUT PIZZA

Emery came to his father one day with another plan in mind.

"Dad," said Emery to Pietro. "Windber school has a basketball scholarship with Concord College in West Virginia, and I want to go to school there. It's about three hours away from here."

"Ok," said Pietro quietly. "You don't want to run the market or the pizza shop, Emerico?"

"It's not that dad," said Emerico. "I just want to get an education."

"Okay, son, okay," said Pietro. "Do what you wish."

Though it broke Pietro's heart to have any of his children away from him, he was so proud of Emery. He and Nicolette and the rest of the family would continue to run the shop although he knew the days without his son would be lonely.

Thankfully he had Nicolette, the pizza shop, and his family and friends to keep him busy. The 1905 building he had purchased so many years earlier from Berwind-White Coal Company was in need of constant repair. Pietro also owned the house on 22nd Street that he had built with his father and rented to local tenants. He would also maintain that property.

D'Arc's Pizza was growing. Every year, Pietro and Nicolette would hire local high school kids to work at the shop along with their friends and family members. It seemed like every time Pietro turned around someone he knew needed a job. He was happy to help them.

The pizza shop was more than just a business to Pietro. It was a family tradition. He started it based on his life-long dream to have something that he could hand down to his family, something that would represent the D'Arcangelo family and the D'Arcangelo name.

Before Pietro knew it, Emery was back from college. He had earned a teaching degree and while he applied for jobs at the Windber School District he would help out in the shop. Emery had also decided to marry his high school sweetheart, Sharon. She lived in the West End of Windber where many Polish, Irish, and Slovakian immigrants settled.

Her mother, Pauline, came from a family of Polish immigrants. She had twelve siblings, and was a gifted cook and homemaker. Sharon's father, Jim, was an Irish smooth-talking car salesman who loved golf. She had two siblings; a sister who was two years older and a younger brother.

Sharon and Emery married in a traditional Catholic ceremony at Saint John's Church in the middle of town surrounded by friends and family.

Linda was in attendance with her husband and now had two daughters, Pietro's first granddaughters.

Emery's wife, Sharon, had worked at D'Arc's Pizza through high school. After graduating she got a corporate job in Johnstown, Pennsylvania at Crown American.

That fall Emery was hired for his first teaching job at Windber High School as a 6th-grade math teacher. That winter Sharon got pregnant with their first child who was due in late October of 1979. Emery and Sharon both worked at their jobs during the day and then at D'Arc's Pizza in the evenings and on weekends.

Pietro gifted Emery the stone house he had built with his father Justino on 22nd Street in Windber. Emery would manage the rentals and tenants and do some renovations on the house so he could live there with his family. At this point, the house was split into three properties. Emery and Sharon would live in the front house with the tenants in the two side properties.

Emery also accepted a position at Windber as the head basketball coach.

The D'Arcangelo family was growing. Linda also had a son who was the first grandson in the D'Arcangelo family. Emery and Sharon had their first daughter, Erica, a few years after that. They then had four more children over the following eight years.

If Pietro wasn't busy enough with the building, store, and pizza shop he now had a growing family of grandchildren. Weekends now included sleepovers where the kids would play games and run curiously around the building, playing outside and in. The tables were full at Sunday dinners and the couches and floors were piled with the family napping after eating.

This was more than Pietro could ever ask for: to watch his children and now his grandchildren grow up and be part of their lives. Each of them also worked at D'Arc's Pizza when they became old enough.

Chapter 14 Recipe
Emery's Pasta Fagioli

Ingredients

2-3 cloves of garlic

1-2 tablespoons of olive oil

1 yellow onion

1 lb spicy ground Italian sausage

4 carrots

4 celery stalks

1 green pepper

2 teaspoons of salt (one for the pasta water)

1 teaspoon of pepper

1 8 oz can dark red kidney beans

1 8 oz can light red kidney beans

1 8 oz can cannellini beans

1 8 oz can tomato paste

1 16 oz can diced tomatoes

1 8 oz can tomato sauce

1 12 oz can of beef broth

1 pound of pasta (Ditalini is recommended)

Directions:

A STORY ABOUT PIZZA

Add olive oil and garlic and onion to a pan and saute on medium heat. Add in your ground sausage, salt and pepper. Once the meat is fully cooked, add in your cut up veggies. Cook the veggies for several minutes until cooked through.

Add in the tomato paste and fry for a few minutes with the veggies. Add in the beef broth, diced tomatoes and sauce. Stir. Turn on low. Open and drain your beans and add them in. Put a lid on the pot and let simmer. If it's too watery add more tomato sauce. If it's too thick, add more broth.

Boil your pasta in a pot with salted water. Drop in pasta, and cook until al dente. Save a little bit of pasta water and drain the rest. Sprinkle in a little bit of parmesan cheese and pasta water to the sauce. Add pasta to a bowl and get a generous portion of the fagioli sauce to put over it.

Add parmesan cheese and hot pepper seeds to the top.

Chapter 15
The Big Move

With Pietro's family growing before his eyes he never thought anything would change. Sunday dinners, mass together, and working together at the pizza shop. His children and grandchildren were close and he had what he always wanted: his family.

D'Arc's Market was scaling down as D'Arc's Pizza had expanded into a full restaurant. The shop still served its famous pizza and sandwiches. It now added salads, more sandwiches, and many different types of pizza to the menu with Pete's daughter-in-law Sharon running the shop.

The shop had a variety of different pizzas with toppings, called specialty pizzas. There was also a special pie named after Pietro's grandson Mike called Mike's Pie.

On Fridays Sharon would bake homemade bread with Nicolette and sell it by the loaf. The next morning Emery and his children would make toast with it and spread butter, homemade jelly, and peanut butter on it.

By now Pietro didn't think anymore about his past years of hardship. He had built the business he had always dreamed of. He was able to provide for the people he loved. Pietro even created a place for his entire family to work and a business they could build their lives around.

That's why when Emery came to talk to him one day he was surprised.

A STORY ABOUT PIZZA

Over the last fifteen years Emery had been a teacher, and a coach at Windber School District. He had also been attending school to gain his Master's Degree.

Pietro had hoped he would stay close to home but just when he thought things would never change, they did.

"Father," said Emery. "I have good news."

"Tell me, son," said Pietro.

"I was offered a job at Somerset School District," he said.

"You're not going to take it," said Pietro. "Do you really want to leave Windber, your coaching position, and your family?"

"Dad, I do," said Emery. "I have five children. I just finished all this education and I have to make more money. They're going to need to go to college. Dad, my wife and I discussed it. We're going to move."

Pietro was silent.

"We're going to leave after the school year," said Emery.

"What about your house?" asked Pietro.

"We're selling it," said Emery.

Pietro could feel his face and ears getting hot. How dare he? After Pietro had worked his entire life to build this for him and his family.

"If you leave," said Pietro. "Don't come back."

Emery's eyes welled up with tears, and he said, "But dad, I thought you would be happy for me."

Pietro walked away.

Though he wanted to support his son, he was heartbroken. He had never wanted his son to leave. Pietro and Emery were having their first fight.

The day of Emery's graduation from his Master's Degree program Pietro showed up and stood in the back. No matter how angry he was with Emery, deep down he was so proud of his son. No matter how proud, he was also stubborn. Pietro left right after the ceremony, and would never tell Emery he had been there.

The following weeks were tough for Emery and Pietro. They still were not speaking. Pietro knew what he had to do. Like any parent, he had to let his son go and support his dreams. Pietro's father, though he loved him, never quite taught him this. But Pietro knew it was the right thing to do. He went to see Emery before he left.

"Knock, knock, Emerico," said Pietro.

"Hi dad," said Emerico.

The two men were silent at first.

"Son, I'm sorry," said Pietro. "My father. He and I never really spoke. It was just assumed that I would be there and I was. And when you decide to leave…"

"I know, dad," said Emery. "I still love you and mom. I would never leave my family, no matter what."

"You were the only one who went to college in our family," said Pietro. "I'm proud of you, son. I'm the most proud I've ever been that you decided to go and get an education. I was never smart enough to do that."

Emery held back tears.

A STORY ABOUT PIZZA

"I love you, dad," he said.

They embraced.

Emery would always have his love and support, no matter what, as would his entire family. Pietro had said his whole life that blood is thicker than water.

That following summer Emery and his family moved away. He started his new job and enrolled his children in the school district where he was working.

Sharon would drive back to Windber on the weekends and work at the pizza shop with the two oldest children.

During that time Emery didn't have a lot of time to visit or work at the shop but the families always met on Sunday for dinner whether at Pietro's or Emery's home.

About a year after Emery and Sharon and their family moved out of Windber, they decided to take a trip. This wasn't like any other summer family vacation that they had gone on. Sharon had spent a number of years working with an educational foundation hosting foreign exchange students. Through this the D'Arcangelo family had several high school students living at their home; a few from Italy.

Emery and Sharon decided they would travel abroad and take Pietro back to Italy to visit the region of Abruzzo. Nicolette, who had grown older and suffered with back problems, was planning to stay in Windber as Pietro, Emery, and Sharon made the journey to Italy.

In the weeks leading up to the trip Pietro was so excited, he couldn't sleep.

He hadn't been in Abruzzo since he was a young boy but still remembered every one of his last moments there. Pietro often wondered what his life would have been like if he stayed in Italy.

Before he knew it he was boarding the plane in Newark, New Jersey on his way to Milan. He would spend a day or two in Milan while Emery and Sharon visited friends, Then a few days in Florence and onto Abruzzo.

Pietro rested, but didn't sleep during the six-hour flight. He got off the plane and went through customs. Then he, Emery, and Sharon got a bite to eat at an auto grill on the way to where they were staying. Even though Pietro wasn't in Abruzzo yet everything there seemed familiar to him. The smell of the bakeries, espresso brewing, people speaking Italian, and locals riding bikes up and down the old stone streets.

Pietro sat at a cafe every morning drinking his espresso and eating a croissant. Some days he had the plain croissant, but others he treated himself to his favorite, creama.

Florence was an even more spectacular site for Pietro than Milan. Pietro, Emery and Sharon walked around the city taking in the sights for days.

Before they knew it, it was time to go to Abruzzo. After a short four-hour ride the three tired but happy travelers drove into Lanciano. Pietro's eyes filled with tears. It was just as he remembered.

Abruzzo, just west of the Adriatic Sea, is known for its fresh seafood. The smell of a fresh catch often filled the streets as fish was sold at the local market. When Pietro arrived in Abruzzo that was one of the first things he smelled. The streets

A STORY ABOUT PIZZA

were fuller, and the market was bigger than he remembered. There were still many locals on bikes but cars and Vespas buzzed quickly up and down the streets.

After a quick walk around the market, Pietro stopped at a pizzeria that looked very similar to one he had frequented as a child. He, Emery, and Sharon enjoyed a few slices and then arrived at the agriturismo to unpack and turn in for a nap.

Though most of Pietro's family had immigrated to the United States nearly sixty years earlier, Pietro had some cousins and relatives who still lived in Abruzzo. One cousin in particular, Carmen, was very close with Pietro. They would reunite that evening speaking Italian for hours and catching up.

As they saw each other for the first time in many, many years the two men embraced and cried tears of joy.

"La mia famiglia," cried Carmen. "It's so good to see you again."

Carmen told Pietro that after Justino and his family moved to America, Justino would send money home to them. The family was able to purchase a few small plots of land where their family homes now sat filled with children and grandchildren.

Pietro woke up early the next morning to meet with Carmen again and enjoy an espresso and croissant together. They walked to the D'Arcangelo family land and Pietro gazed out into the hill as the sun rose. He was happy to be home. Before he knew it, it was time to go back to Windber.

When they returned from Italy, Pietro, Emery, and Sharon returned from the trip, tired but full. Pietro returned to

Nicolette to tell her all about his trip and time with his family and cousin Carmen.

Emery would start back to school that fall and continue with his education.

Soon after, he was promoted to high school principal and had earned a Doctor of Education degree. This time Pietro and Nicolette sat in front at Emery's graduation. Pietro knew that Emery was doing exactly what Pietro did. He was working to better himself so he could take care of his own family.

Emery was then offered another job as a high school Superintendent at a school just outside of Pittsburgh. By this time all five of his children had graduated high school, and all five attended college.

Chapter 15 Recipe
Homemade Bread

Ingredients

5 cups of unbleached flour

2 cups of warm water

½ cup fast rise yeast

A pinch of salt

A pinch of sugar

Directions:

Add flour to a mixer or bowl and hollow out the middle. Add yeast, salt and sugar. Start adding warm water and mix until the dough doesn't stick to your hand or the mixer.

Cover and let rise for about one hour. Take the dough out and use pull and fold to make it into a bread shape. Place the bread in greased bread pans and cover for another 30 minutes to raise.

Bake at 350 for 30 to 40 minutes. Take out of the oven when golden brown. Let sit in a pan to cool.

Chapter 16
A Part of Life

As the days and years passed, and they always do, Pietro grew older and older. He milled around the pizza shop where Nicolette, her sister and brother, his children, and grandchildren were often found working as they sat and talked, laughed, and ate together.

Even though Emery lived forty-five minutes away he, Sharon ,and his children visited often. Even with some of them in college they always made time for one another.

The D'Arcangelo family were very tight-knit. Pietro made sure they spent holidays together and were always loyal to one another. As he said many times, "blood is thicker than water."

Pietro, although he had less energy than usual, was still very active. He was always making sure the pizzas were being made and cooked right. In the winter he manned the coal furnace to keep the building warm. He and Nicolette purchased the house right behind the pizza shop which was just one floor and no stairs, due to Nicolette having trouble going up and down the steps.

Pietro could feel that he was slowing down. The aches and pains in his body affected him more. He was also having a pain in his stomach that wouldn't quite go away. Pietro tried to use a pillow and a brace to keep himself upright but the pain started to become unbearable.

After a trip to his family doctor, Pietro was diagnosed with pancreatic cancer. Due to the advanced forms of the disease,

A STORY ABOUT PIZZA

he decided that surgery would not be the best option. Pietro was now 84 years old.

Like all things that have a beginning, they also have an end. Over the next four months, Pietro struggled with the cancer spreading. During that time he tried to spend as much time with his family as possible.

In the days before his death his entire family gathered at his home. Bedridden, Pietro would lie silently and listen to their voices, their stories, and their laughs.

In his very last moments Pietro looked at his life. All of the trials, the joys, and the pain. The moments when the challenges seemed unbearable to him and the victory of finally persisting to his dream. He had built not just a business but a place he poured his heart and soul into.

This was a place where his family could feel safe. Where they would have each other. Most of all a place where his favorite thing in the world was made: pizza.

Oh, how he loved pizza. From his first slices in Italy to crafting his own recipe in his very own building to share with his family and friends. This was what brought everyone together and kept his family close.

Just as Pietro had lived, he knew that death was a part of life. He closed his eyes and his spirit peacefully left his body.

The tradition of D'Arcangelo's Pizza was carried on by the D'Arc family as it is still family owned and operated for the last sixty-plus years in the small coal-mining town of Windber, Pennsylvania.

- The End -

About the Author

Erica D'Arcangelo is the granddaughter of Pete (Pietro) D'Arcangelo and the firstborn daughter of Emery D'Arcangelo. She was born in Windber, Pennsylvania, and grew up in D'Arc's Pizza Shop along with her parents, four siblings, aunts, uncles, and cousins making and eating pizza before she could walk or talk.

Throughout her life, she was taught about her Italian heritage as she listened to stories from her grandparents and parents even living abroad in Italy at the age of sixteen years old.

Erica is the CEO of a marketing company but, most importantly is a content creator and a storyteller. She was moved by her grandfather's struggle as a Berwind-White coal miner who carried out his life-long dream of opening an Italian pizzeria and family business.

A STORY ABOUT PIZZA

Over the last few years, she has worked with her father for the pizzeria as a marketing manager and content creator on the business's many social media pages and websites.

She resides in the northeast and Tampa Bay area with her husband and daughter.

Printed in the USA
CPSIA information can be obtained
at www.ICGtesting.com
LVHW041133131024
792990LV00019B/78